JOURNEY TO THE CENTRE
OF THE PERSON

JOURNEY TO THE CENTRE OF THE PERSON

Joseph McCarroll

RADIX PRESS
DUBLIN 1986

First published 1986
by Radix Press,
Lebong,
26 Willowfield Avenue,
Goatstown,
Dublin 14, Ireland.

© Joseph McCarroll 1986

Cover design by Patricia Clarke

Typeset by Redsetter Ltd.

Printed by Santry Printing Ltd.

CONTENTS

To my father who taught me how to think,
and to the memory of my mother
who taught me the tales and games of childhood:
together they taught me how to love.

THE SPRINGS OF HUMANKIND

EARTHLINGS

The word 'human', some say, comes from the Latin word *humus*, the earth, soil. In Hebrew also the word for man is *adam* and is closely related to the word for soil, *adamah*. Children of the earth, that is the name we give ourselves. It expresses a universal human experience of a deep, mysterious and important link between us and the earth. The earthlink experience underlies the beautiful custom of placing newborn infants momentarily on the ground, and the strangely apt rite of burying the remains of our dead in the earth. As the space adventure stories have taught us, we are earthlings. The same earthlink experience is present when we name ourselves in the ancient symbolism which speaks of clay being taken and and shaped into human form and brought to life, and when we use the scientific symbolism of a cooling planet which slowly and majestically gives birth to a fantastic sequence of lifeforms culminating in humankind.

THE NAMECALLERS

We are beings who give names to ourselves and we attach great significance to them. This book is about our name, about the search for a name that adequately expresses what we are. The little question Who am I? seems at first to be rather down to earth, but as we delve more and more into it, we find it to be radical, that is to say, it leads us down beneath the surface in search of deep roots, down so far that we have to break through rock; it turns out to be an earth-shattering question. Just think for a moment how intimate our name is to us. To be imprisoned and to have our name taken from us and replaced by a number is to be lessened and hurt, defaced and depersonalised, to be violated. This is because our name is more than a label, it contains and reveals what we are. When our children come in from playing and complain that they are being called names it reminds me of the rhyme my parents gave me to ward off the pain of namecalling: sticks and stones will break my bones, but names will never hurt me. It is not so. The name we give someone expresses what we think and feel about them. And it is the same for our name, it is a symbol of our identity, it expresses our understanding of ourselves and our feelings about ourselves. This is clearly to be seen in the way children love their names. They get tremendous satisfaction out of saying the names that mean a lot to them: Mammy, Daddy, Grandpa, Nana, and their own names. They savour their own names like a sweet. As soon as they begin to write they start signing their name everywhere, on every piece of paper that comes to hand, on their books, on our books, on the wallpaper, with crayons, or worse, with markers! As soon as they get their hands on a type-writer they type, My name is Ingrid, My name is David. At home we have an old dictionary which used to belong to my father. My name is scrawled on it. I remember once as a child finding a patch of newly laid concrete on a building site near home. There was nobody about so I proceeded to inscribe on it my full name and address. Later an irate foreman paid us a visit and had a few words with my father: later still he had a few words with me. To this day I am not sure which annoyed him most, my vandalism, my vanity or my stupidity in leaving the full address. I am inclined to think it was the last.

WHAT'S IN A NAME?

Our name is significant to us because it expresses our identity and because our identity is not something we can take for granted, something that is given to us without problems. It is, rather, something precarious and elusive, something we have to seek out and win, something that has to be built up and protected and sometimes torn down and rebuilt. Our name expresses the identity we have at any given time. In childhood we begin with the name given to us by our family, shortened perhaps to an affectionate nickname. The fact that our name means so much to us tells us something about our-selves. A basic and central drive in us pushes us to seek out and explore what we are and what we are for. Our name expresses the findings of such a quest. A friend of mine was always addressed by his

8

parents by a shortened version of his name. Then he met a girl and she called him by his full name. He switched over to this version of his name: his relationship with her had entered into his identity and altered it. The name by which we choose to be known expresses what we have discovered in these journeys of exploration into our humanity. Another friend is an example of this: he found an important strand of his identity in the national culture so he changed his name and now only answers to the Irish pronunciation of it. For us human beings, to be is to become, and the key to our development is the quest in which we discover what we are and what we are for. This suggests to us how we should live so as to unfold and fulfil our humanity.

IN SEARCH OF OUR ORIGIN

We seek many things, food, money, fame and so on, but we rarely name ourselves after any of these. The way we do name ourselves reveals to us that one of the most powerful urges in us is the primeval drive to return to our origin, to find the source of our being. As the compass needle turns spontaneously to the north, we go in search of our beginnings, our ground. We puzzle ourselves and to discover what we are and what we are for, we go in search of our origin. Our name ties us to our family and so we turn there to discover who we are; here the precious gift of grandparents to grandchildren has its place as those who have the time to talk, speak of the past to those who have the time and the wonder to listen.

HUMANKIND

We are aware that we are unfinished, fragile and yet most valuable. We wonder what we are for and this leads us to ask what we are from. In other times the words 'man' and 'mankind' seemed adequate to express what we are. Today, however, there is a new appreciation of the equal humanity of women and some find these words unsuitable, as if mankind excluded women. This development in sensitivity calls for a refinement of language, a new name. To acknowledge the full and equal humanity of women I have chosen the beautiful word 'humankind' for the mysterious extended family of which we are all, men and women, full members. This book is an account of a personal exploration undertaken by me and shared with you to invite you to do likewise; I address you directly rather than talk impersonally about he, she or one; and to avoid the awkward he/she I write about us and what we have in common.

A RIOT OF RESURRECTIONS

Spring is the season of new beginnings, of beginning again. The delicate layer of life that embroiders the land stirs and awakens from the deathlike sleep of winter. A riot of resurrections ripples around the countryside. At the sun's bidding the happy-go-lucky rite of spring recommences yet again. In this lighthearted liturgy miracles are a dime a dozen. On all sides bare branches burst into bud. Tiny green shoots pierce the brown soil like the soldiers who sprang from the dragon's teeth: I picture them like toy soldiers standing stiffly to attention, their spears held by their sides so that their spearheads would have broken first through the clay. The emergence of these green spearheads shows that magic is on the loose. A grace of growth brings life to everything it touches. The number and liveliness of the flecks of new growth seem at first glance like a chaotic rush, but there are a million methods in this madness. It is only the apparent chaos of complexity like the frenetic preparations for a circus. The pulse of the earth has been quickened by sunfire and its heart beats faster.

THE SECRET OF SPRING

The earth's celebration of the spring mystery reaches its climax in the arrival of the flowers. They are the finale of the festival of life reborn and from them we may learn the secret of spring. Here is a crocus with a rich yellow bloom. It sticks up out of the ground, a splinter broken off the sun and shot down into the earth like a bolt of gold. Nearby a blue crocus, a splinter of heaven; the sky has fallen. This is the secret of spring. The sun has come down to share its life of light with the earth. Different flowers capture and display different parts of the light, like that red tulip. Some can hold all the light and are white. The fragile, fleeting snowdrop stands with head bowed, radiant with the secret of spring. Its matchless amalgam of elegance, simplicity and modesty proclaims that the role of the earth is to wait, to be open, to receive what comes from the sun. You might think that any fool could grasp that the point of the carnival of spring is that the sun has come down to share its light-life with the earth. But we humans are dimmer than the dullest ditchwater: we have been known to miss the most obvious points. For this very reason the season lays on a special Mad Hatter's tea party to make it clear, even to us, what is happening in spring. Clumps of daffodils with their brilliant yellow and white flowers sway backwards and forwards in the breeze. Who can look at these amazing flowers without being reminded of cups, saucers and plates, or more appropriately, of chalices, golden goblets and silver platters? This swaying feast invites us to participate in the springs of the earth.

SLEEPING BEAUTY

We are the children of the earth so it is only natural that the springs of the earth enkindle in us an urge to springs of our own, the springs of humankind. I have written these pages as a travel journal and the journey they recount is one which springs out of my own deepening conviction that in the closing years of the second Christian millennium we are frozen in a long winter of discontent so thorough as to be a new ice age. It is said that when the Roman soldiers saw Ireland surrounded in mists and clouds they named it Hibernia, Winterland. Different mists and clouds enfold us now and a more deathly winter, and it is to go beyond them and find new springs of humankind that the journey plotted in these pages is undertaken. Over and over again the year re-enacts the story of Sleeping Beauty. The sun-prince awakens the sleeping beauty of the earth with the soft kiss of spring light. The springs of the earth speak powerfully to the children of the earth and call forth from us springs of our own. In each of us beauty sleeps, cast into coma by curses. Talents buried by avalanches of cynicism, manipulation and compromise, untouched and untried for so long that their whereabouts and even their very existence are forgotten. All that remains is a vague recollection of what we once knew ourselves to be. The way we live draws on only a fraction of who we are. We go about our daily business like sleep-walkers, alive, but only just, only a little. To remember what we have lost, to long for the long-forgotten, to lift the spell, to find a lost treasure of the human person, is to bring about in our life a spring.

THE UNFINISHED BUSINESS OF AN ICE AGE

As long as the evil queen reigns, snow and ice cover the land and winter never ends. Whenever she comes across people enjoying life and befriending one another she screams a curse, waves her wand and turns them into stone, freezing them in the middle of different actions like statues of ice. As soon as her power is broken the ice starts to thaw, the snow melts and spring begins at last. The frozen tableaux come back to life and finish the actions which they had been doing when she petrified them. Every day we write a page of the story of our life and on any page something can go wrong; a great wrong done to us, or by us, sets off an ice age in us. Once such an ice age has occurred it has to be put right. It will not just go away or get better by itself. Until we are healed it remains and whatever we were doing at the time is frozen in mid-flight within us. We usually try to ignore the pages of ice in our past because it hurts so much to face and fight them, but if we leave them there then we build the rest of our life on ice and risk its collapse. Such an ice age takes out of circulation precious facets of our personality and puts them into suspended animation. They become frozen assets. When the spell is lifted they re-enter our experience and enrich our lives. A new spring bubbles into our consciousness and what was written on that frozen page is remembered, responded to and written into our living present.

SKATING

Of course we do not want to delve into these cold corners of our character. We want to let sleeping dogs lie. We pretend that while lots of the people we know carry with them the wounds of their past, we are somehow exempt. When I think of this a painting comes to mind. It shows a town scene. The river has frozen over and people are playing on the ice. Adults and children are skating. Perhaps someone is lighting a fire. They seem to be having a good time, but it leaves me uneasy. Don't they realise that they are on ice? What if it cracks? It is their care-free attitude that troubles me. I would be more at ease if they showed some awareness of the precariousness of their situation. Our lives are like this. Forced gaiety and desperate efforts at amusement disguise a deep anxiety about the foundations upon which our lives and our society are built. We feel in our bones that something is awfully wrong but we are too terrified to look down and see what it is. But we have to respect this bonefeeling and yield to it. We have to recognise that the foundations on which we have built the modern world are ice not stone, and we have to dismantle them and sink them far far deeper, below the layers of ice in bedrock. We have to stop skating on the surface of our humanity and break the ice.

IN SEARCH OF SECOND CHILDHOOD

As I cast about for images to express what I am trying to find, memories of childhood, its stories and games, flood into my mind. I feel that in childhood I had a wholeness of vision, an openness, a responsiveness, a receptivity to the whole of reality which, somehow, I have lessened and lost. Perhaps it is that the water is purest nearest the spring, and that as it flows down it is contaminated from all sides by pollutants.

Children seem to me more alive than many adults. Certainly this is the most precious gift that my children have given me: each of them is a delicate and devastating reminder of what I am, of what I have lost. The spontaneity, the liveliness, the exuberance, the energy, the serious playfulness, the sheer joy in being alive — all these move me deeply to search for the lost order of my own existence. The outrageous, inexhaustible, bubbling fountain of questioning and affection that each of them is, has taught me how much of my humanity I have submerged and frozen alive since I graduated into adulthood.

To make myself one with my children I have not had to lose anything so as to get down to their level. Far from it: I have had to grow, to retrieve a morsel of the integral humanness that comes so easily to them. Childhood, with its vivaciousness and innocence, its integrity and vulnerability symbolises for me the full humanity for which I am searching.

We are at once, too big and too small. Before Alice could get into Wonderland she had to change her size in two ways: we must do likewise. Even to see in through the door we have to get down on our knees. We have become too big. Our desires for money and power, for pleasure and comfort, for fame and success, for property and entertainment, have bloated our hearts. We have to lose this deadweight if we are ever to fit through the little door into full and mature personhood. Like Alice, we have to cry mightily so that our tears may flush out the many monsters that lurk in the dark depths of us. We are greater than we have been led to believe: we need to realise and seize that greatness. But to do so requires of us that we cultivate a proper human littleness, training with the practice, the struggle and the discipline that characterise the preparation for a marathon.

13

I am in search of second childhood. To the closed and stunted deformation that passes for normal adulthood in our society, this search and its goal seem childish and odd. The secret of second childhood is the discovery that open-ended growth is the normal state for an adult. We have been tricked into thinking that once we reach adulthood we should not grow any further. Although the body reaches full maturity half way through our lifespan, we as persons should never stop growing. As the earth undergoes spring after spring, so, too, should we. There is no end to the springs of humankind.

DEEP SELF DIVING

The surface of the lake of our being is frozen over. To those on the surface the film of ice seems very thick, but it is only paper-thin in comparison to the depth of the lake. Beneath the surface are lost treasures, held captive often by monsters that lurk in the lower darkness. To dive down into the depths of our being, to face and slay the monsters that live there, to find and bring up these lost treasures of the human person, this is truly to initiate a splendid new beginning in our life, a spring of humankind. This book is an invitation to break the ice and engage in some deep self diving. No search for lost treasure would be complete without a map and some mysterious clues, and that is what these pages provide. Whether you undertake the journey is entirely up to you. Nobody can force you to do it. You can read these pages without deciding to break through the ice of your own life and explore your depth. Then you will read this book as a travel journal that relates what I did. If you do not dive into the depth of your own being then you will never find the treasures that lie hidden there, you will never encounter and defeat the monsters that sulk there, you will know about these matters only at second hand.

SECRET IDENTITY

The greatest treasure that lies in wait for us is the discovery of our true identity. The question that begins the journey to the Centre of the person is Who am I? To ask this question, really ask it personally, is to take the first step on the journey to the Centre of the person. But what is it that makes us ask that question in this way? Another children's story comes to mind. The king's child lived in a little cottage deep in the forest with the wood-cutter and his wife. This tale of a secret identity enchants. Something deep in us identifies with the child and longs to share the adventure to which the secret identity will surely lead. This is because we too are more than we seem. Each of us has a secret identity beneath our ordinary life. Each of us is called to some great destiny, to a fantastic future in which we marry into a royal family and live happily ever after. Like the super-heroes in the comics we have to discover our powers and our secret identity. Only then can we be sure what our mission is and undertake it regardless of what adventures and dangers it brings. Only in this way can we fulfil our destiny and head for Journey's End.

JOURNEY TO THE CENTRE OF THE PERSON

This book, then, presents a journey to the Centre of the person. It is a definite journey towards a clearly named destination. The starting point is the question Who am I? This initial question broadens out into several questions: Is there more to me than meets the eye? What makes me more than an animal? And finally, What am I for? The destination is an understanding of the human person. But how, you may wonder, can what I have found out about myself be of any use or relevance to you? You are not me, our lives and experiences differ: we have not even met. What is to be gained by sharing the experience and exploration of another person? The answer lies in the universal childhood expressed in that word 'another': I am another person like you. Each of us is a spring of humankind. You are free to take whatever you choose from these pages. As you read them, what count are the points that ring a bell, that you recognise as valid for your experience. Each of these points in common is like one of the readings that a scientist takes, it goes down on the graph-paper as another dot. As more and more readings are taken and added to the paper a pattern begins to emerge on the paper until at last the scientist grasps the pattern and joins up the dots to form a graph which shows the relationship behind the readings.

What you take out of these pages are the points that ring true for you. You map them out and join them up to show what you are, your secret identity. In children's comics there is always a dot-to-dot puzzle: a confusion of dots each with a number. When we join them up in the right order a picture emerges. As you note the points that truly express your experience and relate them to one another you are drawing an outline of yourself, you are signing your autograph, you are discovering your real name, your identity.

EARTH DEPTH

1

You, Earth, you are our home for now,
Not a hostile rock on which we're cast;
You are a cosmic poem of human personhood,
A metaphor of man written vast.

2

You, like us, have a depth beneath your surface,
You have a life below your land,
You have a fire at your centre,
A treasure in the cup of your hand.

3

You who are fire at heart but housed in stone
Are drawn to that which is pure fire alone.
Full explosion, fire through and through,
Such is the Centre sought by the centre in you.

4

The spark to the blaze is drawn as same to Same,
The spark seeking consummation in the Flame.

CHAPTER I

PERSON-DEPTH

To begin the journey to the Centre of the person ask yourself this question, Who am I? At the beginning of every year perhaps you fill in the opening pages of a new diary: name, address, telephone number at home and at work, next of kin. At the end is the place for the addresses and telephone numbers of the important people in your life. The information in your diary is private, in other words, it is related to your own personal life. Here you should find a clue to the answer to the initial question, Who am I? But is it not true that this information is somehow external to you: someone else could memorise all the facts in it about you but they would not have really penetrated to the innermost you. That information would tell them about what you are like on the outside, not on the inside. In fact, none of these bits of information by themselves, nor all of them taken together, are you: you are more than them. If you moved to a new job, you would still be yourself. True, something would change, but something more central would be the same. The same goes for a change of home or friends. We find that the very aspects of ourselves which came to mind when we groped around for an answer to the question Who am I? do not get to the core of our being but provide expressions of this core. My home, for instance, expresses what I am but is not identical with it: I am more than my home, and although it would hurt me considerably to lose it, the loss of my home would not bring about the end of me. This first attempt at pinning down who I am, then, shows that while it is easy enough to list my external characteristics, my job, my social class, my political affiliation, my nationality, and so on, none of these can be simply identified with me. Who I am slips through this list.

Often our society seems to us to be like a gigantic machine in which we are nothing more than cogs, replaceable units: if I break down, I can be replaced by someone else who can do the job just as well. The experience of being treated as nothing more than a cog sends a shudder through us. There are several other areas in our lives where we are treated as nothing more than . . . and we feel this as a belittling, a hurt. What happens in these instances is that one of the external aspects of our being is taken by others as if it were the whole of us with nothing left over, and we know at once that this is mistreatment. I have often had a similar apprehension where television scientists describe the process of evolution and give the impression that it is an uncontestable conclusion of modern science that we human beings are nothing more than higher animals, products of blind evolution driven by chance. The question Who am I? springs from experiences of feeling threatened or suffocated by those who push me to regard myself as nothing more than a member of their group, their family, their social class, their state or nation, their ethnic or cultural tradition, their club or movement, their political party, their social clique. Whenever a 'they' tries to pressurise me into feeling or acting as if I were nothing more than a part of their group, my uniqueness and integrity as a human being is violated.

Today the intimate and private zone of personhood is under siege from a horde of wild '-isms'and '-ologies' which seek to quench its unique flame. Seducers and pressurisers try to get us to put on this or that strait-jacket of conformity to a false view of personhood which reduces us to nothing more than a part of a greater whole. Slogans that sound open turn out to be the warcries of closed groups: they seem to summon everyone, but they turn out to be banners that unite some against others. If we want a universal call, then let it be to all human beings: persons of the world unite! Let us exclude nobody, young or old, rich or poor, male or female, ill or well, clever or stupid, normal or abnormal, born or unborn, handicapped or independent.

The initial question Who am I? is a first step away from all those who would reduce us to nothing more than parts of their group or some process. It directs us to explore what we mean by the word 'person'. Despite all the external differences that place us in this or that group, we are all persons: what then is a person?

The word 'person', some say, is made from the Latin *per,* meaning 'through', and *sonare,* meaning 'to sound'. It calls to mind the ancient actors' masks each with its formal set expression, like the happy and sad faces that are found hanging around the stage in a theatre. When he had a particular mask on him, the actor had to play that character.

The word 'person', then, reminds us that a human being always comes before us with a particular external presentation, but we have to keep in mind that there is more in that person than is manifested through that mask: other masks would reveal other aspects of that person. In the human being, thus, there is always this mysterious interplay between inner and outer, between the some that meets the eye, and the more that lies hidden beneath.

And we human persons not only have to wear many faces, we have to make new ones as we grow. And since human growth should be unending throughout our lifetime, each face we 'put on' is never more than a provisional and imperfect revelation of us. There is an ongoing struggle in each of us between old achievement and new discovery. At any point in time we have a particular character and way of life which is embodied in many routines. This expresses and embodies what we understand about ourselves. When a new discovery occurs it upsets the balance and demands some dismantling and transformation of our routines, our way of living and even our character.

I AM A MYSTERY

We are strange beings. We found that to answer the question, Who am I? it was not enough to list external aspects because if these were changed I would still be myself. We found that the word person was appropriate because it suggests the presence behind the external aspects of an inner centre which builds and directs them so as to express and embody itself in them. It is precisely because of this 'more' hidden behind what appears, that we have found it necessary to undertake a journey of self-exploration which begins with these outer aspects and travels in to discover their source. In the very act of breaking through the surface and beginning to dive below, our first question, Who am I? is changed into its second form, Is there more to me than meets the eye? and it is this form of the question which governs the present stage of the journey. And the answer to this second form of the question is yes, a resounding yes, that is to say, a yes which sounds out through the many masks of personhood in many different ways. We have all had the experience of acting differently with different people and feeling that no single action of ours fully expresses all that we have within us. What are we, then, that we can be so different with different people? We are mysteries. When I look back over the last fifteen years of my own journey to the Centre of the person what strikes me most forcibly is how much I had underestimated my being: I have found that I am far far more than I had expected. If I were asked to sum up my findings over that time in one phrase I would say that I have discovered that I am a mystery, that there is more to me than meets the eye. This discovery is the first major milestone on the journey to the Centre of the person: each of us is a mystery, the human person is a mystery. What does this mean? What exactly is a mystery? A mystery has seven characteristics:

1. It is something that is there, something we can see or sense in some way.
2. We are aware that it is present.
3. It has a meaning.
4. We are aware that it has a meaning.
5. We do not yet know what this meaning is.
6. We are aware that we do not yet know what the meaning is.
7. We are very drawn or attracted by this meaning that lies beyond our grasp.

A mystery, then, is a known unknown. Now, it is in this precise sense that each of us is a mystery. And not only a mystery to others. First and foremost, each of us is a mystery to himself or herself, and we should protect the air of mystery that hangs around the human person from pollution just as enthusiastically as we protect the air we breathe. But something has gone terribly wrong. We have forgotten that we are mysteries. We take ourselves for granted. We act as though each of us is a finished product, a fact. We have lost the sensitivity to the mysteriousness of ourselves and of the others. A numbness of mind and heart has seized us and rendered us unable to appreciate and respect the mystery of the human person. This numbness is as dangerous for our personhood as bodily numbness is for our physical safety and health. If my arm is numb and I do not notice this, then I may damage myself because if it gets cut or hurt or twisted I will feel nothing. In the same way if we have lost the consciousness of the human person as a mystery then we may mistreat ourselves and one another and never notice the damage. Because of the concussion which we have sustained at the hands of the '-isms' and '-ologies' which tell us that we are nothing more than parts of the social machine, or nothing more than cannon-fodder for the revolution, or nothing more than animals, and so on, we are suffering from an amnesia, a memory loss, regarding the real nature of the human person. Here, then, is the next step to be taken in the journey to the Centre of the person, the recovery of the sensitivity to the mysteriousness of the human person. Modern society teaches us to become closed to the full reality of what we are as human persons. We have to a great extent swallowed this false way of regarding ourselves, hook, line and sinker. The way to recover from this concussion, this amnesia, is to give long consideration to this possibility: Is there more to you than meets the eye? Do you think of yourself as a mystery? Do you treat yourself as a mystery? Are you willing to give serious consideration to the possibility that you could be suffering from a numbness which blinds you to what you are? Are you willing to go further, to spend a while trying to awaken a fuller sensitivity to the full range of your being? If this numbing has taken place then you will feel sceptical or cynical about all this talk about you being a mystery. Nonetheless,, the truth is that you are a magical well, a mysterious well of infinite depth, a holy well, perhaps. Do you dare to go down deep into the well of your being in search of the spring of your personhood? You will find that you are a thirst, an emptiness, in search of utter quenching. Would such a quest, such a finding, be worthwhile?

JACK-IN-THE-BOX, JILL-IN-THE-BOX

One of the facts about us which shows that we are not facts is the way we continually go beyond what we have already reached. This is remarkably clear in children. They ask questions endlessly: they seem to have bottomless pits of energy for play, and in particular for running around the home and shouting at the top of their voices. But it is no less true for us adults. Nothing satisfies us. We struggle for years to reach a goal and when we get there we find that it does not still the search of our being for more. We sense that we are as yet unfinished and we long for fulfilment. Is this not true for you? Do you want to remain forever just as you are at this moment? Or are there things you have to do, to finish, to set right, to make? Behind these projects is there not in you a drive that pushes imperiously towards . . . Towards what? Well, at least we can say, towards something like fulfilment or perfection, whatever that may consist in. This drive shows in our abhorrence of imperfection and breakdown, failure and closure. We may not be too clear about what we want to become, but we usually have a very sharp idea of who we do not want to turn out like: that Aunt with the cold manner, that teacher who crushed questioning. We are an urge to be more and more fully. When we begin to follow this line of inquiry we suddenly feel a chill. A wave of horror can sweep over us as we get a flash of dread about where the search may lead us. Supposing, we whisper to ourselves, we find that we are for something we cannot reach! It is no accident that this particular anxiety should rise up and try to scare us off the path and force us to turn back and abandon our journey. Part of this dread comes from our awareness that the way of life and of looking — at the human being which modern society and its experts offer, have — drummed into us is that we are nothing more than . . . and so we should be satisfied with little. To face the full enormity of our being and the outrageous size of our thirst pushes us to accept that we shall have to go beyond our modern way of living and thinking in order to find something immense enough to fill us. Another part of this dread is the candle's terror of a wind so great that it could extinguish its tiny flame, and we shall come back to that later. For the moment, however, we have to regain sensitivity to the full range of human striving. It seems that we want everything, the whole universe, all being. This was brought home to me vividly the other day by a game that our children were playing at breakfast. 'What would you wish for if you had three wishes?', one began. 'I'd wish for a million other wishes', said the other, 'And when the last of those wishes was reached, I'd wish for another million wishes.' The other took up the idea, 'And every time I got to the last wish, I'd wish for more wishes.' One of them even wanted to take precautions against forgetting to renew her wishes. 'I wouldn't leave it till the last wish in case I forgot to ask for more wishes.' It was only a children's game, but in it I could sense the unlimited thrust of human striving. The phrase that ran through my mind was: there is nothing they would not want if they could have it. When we begin to regain a little of the realisation of just how gigantic is the true reach of the human person, we express this discovery in some such phrase as, There is nothing on earth that would fully satisfy us. It was this noble passion for going beyond that really underlay the amazing space race and especially the race to put a man on the moon. Reluctantly we are compelled to admit that nothing in the world can still the storm of seeking that rages in the human heart. One of the deepest and most passionate thinkers of the twentieth century was Albert Camus. He never seemed to break clearly with the atheism or at least the agnosticism which he saw as the dominant climate of Western thought and sensitivity. He was able, nonetheless, to rediscover the full range of human longing, and in particular its world-transcending intention. In *The Myth of Sisyphus** he recognises that in man there is a desire for the infinite whereas the universe is only finite and so unable to satisfy human longing. Each of us is like a Jack-in-the-box, or lest there be any hint of bias, a Jill-in-the-box. Within us we find a tension to go beyond, to transcend, what we have already reached. This inbuilt longing for more pushes us like a spring to go beyond any and every finite achievement in search of more. Like a Jack-in-the-box, each of us is driven by an inner spring to leap out through a secret trap-door onto the roof of the world in search of something large enough to answer the call of our humanity. We human persons, then, are transcenders, go-beyonders; each of us is a Jack-in-the-box or a Jill-in-the-box whose innermost desire is to open and flower, to reach beyond every limited and restricted fulfilment for further fulness. On the human heart, on the human mind, one word is written, open.

EDDIE'S SONG

To talk of opening and flowering could mislead some people into thinking that human fulfilment is only possible for the few who are well-off materially and healthy in body and feelings. I have always felt a special revulsion against those approaches to human development which were accessible only to the select few, the rich, the brilliant, the healthy or any other subsection of the great unwashed humankind. I suppose this kind of attitude revolts me because I find vestiges of it in myself and have to fight against them all the time. I call this type of view the Club of the Beautiful People: it means that as far as the members of the clique are concerned only those fortunate enough to have the required characteristic are allowed to join. These are the beautiful people: the rest of humanity is consigned to the outer darkness and does not matter. It is important to test any proposed new view of the human person and of how we should live against a hard case rather than in terms of how well it suits the beautiful people. My hard case is Eddie.

Eddie is a friend of mine who died a few years ago before reaching thirty years of age. When he was a child the doctors found that he was suffering from muscular dystrophy of a progressive and eventually fatal type. He became more and more incapacitated until he was unable to do anything at all for himself. Here, you might think, was a young man who could not mature as a human person or have a fully human life. He could do nothing. He was unable to pursue a career, get married and have a family, play sports or drive a car. He was not even able to look after himself in the elementary things like eating, drinking and dressing. He was utterly dependent on his parents and friends. However, he did grow as a human person. When I met him, towards the end of his life, he had been through several crises in which he had struggled to find the meaning of his strange life of helplessness. I would have to say that he was one of the happiest people I have ever met, and it was not a superficial, hail-fellow-well-met extroversion but an inner calm, a striking peacefulness. He was acquainted with suffering of the severest kind and yet there was in him a tranquility.

When you met him first you stretched out your hand to say hello: he was unable to move his hand in response. You felt pity. How awful for him. You wanted to do something for him, to give him something. When you left, however, you were aware that you had been enriched by meeting him. To be with him was to see things in the right perspective, and that meant to appreciate the primacy of the person over everything else. You might think that because he was unable to fend for himself he would not be able to help anyone else. But this was not the case. Eddie found an ideal to live by, an ideal that stood the test of making sense of his situation of total helplessness, severe disease and early death. His ideal was to become perfect in love. His ideal, his model, was a man on a cross who seemed powerless and unable even to move but who in that very moment loved most powerfully and effectively. The really challenging thing about Eddie was that he knew exactly what he was about. Many people came to him. He said about this, 'All I do is make myself one with them and listen, really listen.' He saw that his role was to be like the root of the tree, hidden and immobile and yet giving life to the rest. He understood that it was his role to be there for the others, there to listen and to love, and he did this devastatingly. Each person who came received his undivided attention. He had understood that there is only one thing which is absolutely worth doing, that is worth doing even in the face of meaningless death and suffering, and that is to love perfectly in the present moment. After a visit to him you found yourself asking, 'Is my life filled with actions as worthwhile as his?' His life was a confident statement of the burning conviction that measured against death only love is unambiguously worthwhile. Eddie was one of the most developed persons I have ever met. Whenever I hear people propose an ideal for human living and growth I think of Eddie and I ask whether the ideal they are offering would have made as much sense of his life as his ideal did.

Before he died Eddie wrote a last letter. It was to the mother of the man on the cross. Eddie saw her as the expert in the nothingness which he was living as his life drew to a close. After he died his friends made this letter into a song. One phrase from it has haunted me as I have been working on these pages. It expresses his acceptance of his being nothing and its meaning: 'Happy to be an open flower'.

OPEN, SESAME!

When Ali Baba speaks the secret password 'Open, Sesame!' the rock of the mountainside which had seemed so solid opens out and there before him lies the fabulous treasure. A secret password has been engraved on each of us also and if we discover it and utter it properly then the solid rockface of our routine cracks and crumbles, and underneath we find the fabulous riches of the human person that we are and should become. There is in each of us an inner command to open and to flower. This is the fundamental thrust of our mind and heart towards being. This basic call of our being for more and more being is a call to opening. How many closed ways of feeling, behaving, thinking and relating tangle up our lives: we are called to open these knots. How many adventures await us behind closed doors, secret doors: we are called to open them. What a story lies untold within us, an inner plan written on our mind and heart waiting to be told in our life: we are called to open this flower of personhood.

If there really is more to me than meets the eye, more even than meets my eye, then as soon as I begin to realise the presence of this 'more' it becomes a matter of the utmost urgency to explore and chart it. After an accident we have to do physiotherapy, special exercises designed to help us regain lost sensitivity. We have suffered a concussion, a memory loss, a numbness about the full reality of our personhood: we need to do exercises which will restore in us a full appreciation of what we are as human persons. We need passwords which can break open the solid rockface of our routine, our way of living, even perhaps our character, and reveal to us the treasures that lie within. In particular we find it hard to take seriously the suggestion that we are in some way infinite, unlimited. So drastically have we been interfered with by the dominant way of life imposed by our society that we find it ridiculous to hold that each human person is in any real sense infinite. Perhaps you do not believe that there is nothing in the world that could bring you complete satisfaction. Well then, try to envisage what would bring you total unending fulfilment. It could not be any one of the things that we find in the world because we need so many of them just to survive. Again, our needs are recurrent so we would need a series of each type of thing. But beyond that can you glimpse the frightening fact that because each of us is more than all these limited goods, none of them, nor even all of them, could bring total fulfilment that would never end to us? If not, can you at least observe in your own experience that you have not reached this state of completion and perfect happiness? And if we feel that it is too much to say that there is in each of us a something which is infinite, can you at least feel that death seems to ruin any chance which the things of the world have to bring us everlasting satisfaction? We are starting from a position of damaged sensitivity concerning the full range of our longing. It should not come as a surprise to us that we find it hard at first to believe how immense we really are. We have to think about this suggestion for a while. To tease out its implications, to let it sink in. We need time to explore the difference which such a self-understanding would make to the way we live. The idea that we might be infinite in some way is like a jack-in-the-box: this toy celebrates the joy of surprise; the parents give it to the child and enjoy the child's surprise when, as soon as he opens the lid, the little clown pops up and out on the end of a spring. The child then runs back to the parents and makes them open it: they pretend to be hugely surprised and the child gets great satisfaction from their shock. And we enjoy the child's enjoyment of our surprise. The possibility that each of us as a human person is in some way infinite, then, is like a jack-in-the-box: we have to play around with it and explore its meaning. We will find that the more we ponder it, the more sense it makes of many different aspects of our experience: and this is the mark of a true idea, that it makes sense of our experience, that it rings true. We will begin to feel how this view of ourselves gives us enough room to breathe, frees us from a cramped, constrained feeling which only now we begin to notice. The passwords which are most effective in opening up our sensitivity to our true dimensions are questions. We have begun with the question, Who am I? and it has extended into the question, Is there more to me than meets the eye? Now we are shifting the emphasis of the question a little, hoping to get more light by coming at the same problem from a different angle. Now we are asking, What am I? and, How much more is there in me than meets the eye? We are infinite not in achievement, not in fact, not in our power to satisfy the thrust of our humanity: we are infinite in potential, in what we can desire, in capacity for longing. Even this desire, this longing, is not present in us as infinite all at once: no, we desire first one thing, then another, and after that another, and so on. And this 'and so on', the three dots which indicate continuation without end $(2, 4, 6, 8, \ldots)$ are hints of what we mean by our infinity. It is not that we do at this moment actually desire everything: it is more that our experience shows a relentless going beyond which carries us always one step further than previous best achievement. Is there some beauty which you would not like to behold and enjoy? Is there some vital truth which you would wish to have concealed from you? Is there some good thing in the universe which you would like to be withheld from you? Is there some unity which you would wish to break or never to understand? And if there are such limits to your striving, do you not feel that they are in you as wounds to be healed rather than maturities that make you glad? Questions like these help us to plumb the depth of our longing.

PERSON-DEPTH

Like oil, like coal, like diamonds, like pearls, the treasure of the human person lies not on the surface but beneath in the hidden depth. Like the riches of the sea, the riches of the human person are only to be reached by diving. Like the riches of the earth, the riches of personhood have to be mined. Our being as human persons is well-being. To remain fully human we must continually draw up more to the surface from the depth below, otherwise the surface turns into dead stone. The human person is an amazing kind of being: there is more to each of us than meets the eye, even our own eye. We are like icebergs: only a tiny fraction is visible, the greater part is hidden below the surface. Each of us is a mystery, not only to one another, but in an urgent and primordial sense, to ourself. The more-than-meets-the-eye of the human being is person-depth. Today our awareness of the existence of the hidden inner reality of the human being is largely blunted by the way of living and of seeing people which is dominant. This way of life and of seeing people has possessed us so thoroughly that we find it frankly silly to suggest that every single person is of immense significance. When we are pushed we may grudgingly admit that there are several aspects of each person which we do not know, but our overall feeling is that we do know the basics about the people we meet every day; we feel we know all that matters about them. In fact it is rather threatening to be asked to consider that this might not be the case, that we might have missed the most important thing, not only about our friends, relations and acquaintances, but even about ourselves. Nonsense, we feel. But if it is true that each of us is a person-depth, then we have to rethink everything. The way we live, the way we treat other people, the way we educate our children, the way we order society, all these at present are so designed that they reflect the dominant belief that there is no person-depth in each human being. If there is, they will all have to be dismantled and rebuilt in accordance with the true dimensions of human personhood. If we really do have a person-depth beneath the surface of our lives, then the way of living which has been worked out and embodied over the past centuries is wrong in depth and squashes us into a lifestyle which deforms and damages us. We are like jack-in-the-boxes which have never been opened, like sane people enclosed in strait-jackets. Because we do not recognise the radical openness of the human person we put up with a world which denies this openness and restricts and hems us in on all sides. Each of us is a well of infinite wishing; the dominant way of life today mistreats us as if we were nothing more than puddles.

JACK AND JILL, GIANT-KILLERS

If there really is a person-depth in each of us then we are in a situation like that of Jack in the story: someone gave him a bean and told him that it had amazing properties. He did not believe them and threw it away. Next morning he discovered that it had grown into a beanstalk which stretched up into the air out of sight. He climbed the stalk and discovered a land in the sky where there were extraordinary things which could satisfy his heart's desire. But they were guarded by a giant who wanted to eat Jack so he had to slay the giant. We, too, have neglected the seed of our personhood and disbelieved in its amazing qualities: we have thrown our humanity to one side. We have been devoured by a giant who promises to give us in return all that we need to satisfy our heart's desire. But the giant of modern society lies: we give our lives to this monster but receive little or nothing in return in the way of personal flowering or even respect and care. Contemporary society takes us and uses us like instruments for its own ends and when we are used up it throws us aside like waste. We have to slay this giant, or at least to free ourselves sufficiently from its grip to sow the seed of our being and watch it grow to its full height: only by allowing its full reach to our being will we have in front of our very eyes the evidence that we need to convince us that the giant's claims are false, that modern society cannot give us what it promises, namely, some kind of heaven on earth, some kind of adequate human fulfilment. Every Jack and Jill of us needs to become a giant-killer in order to gain the opportunity to plant and cultivate the bean of our personhood, and especially to discover the incredible stretch of our humanity. If we are a person-depth then we will have to leave room for this hidden dimension to flourish in the way we arrange our lives and our society. And how much room we leave will depend on just how deep we believe our person-depth to be.

AN ENCLOSED VIEW OF HUMANKIND AND OF THE WORLD

It may help in moving towards a clearer understanding of the implications of recognising our person-depth if we look more closely at *The Myth of Sisyphus*, the book by Albert Camus, which I mentioned earlier. He explored the human person and found that there was something in us which is too large for the world: he called the situation of humankind in the world 'absurd' because he found that we just do not fit into the world, it is not big enough for us, we reach beyond it, we seek more than the world has to offer. He found in us an infinite desire for meaning and value, while he found in the universe only a limited meaning and value: therefore, the world is too small to satisfy us. He says that 'to understand is above all to unify.' 'The mind's deepest desire', he continues, 'is an insistence upon familiarity, an appetite for clarity.' 'That nostalgia for unity, that appetite for the absolute, illustrates the essential impulse of the human drama' (p. 21). 'But what is absurd is the confrontation of the irrational [by which he means the world which is not infinitely intelligible] and the wild longing for clarity whose call echoes in the human heart' (p. 24). 'He feels within him his longing for happiness and for reason. The absurd is born of this confrontation between the human need and the unreasonable silence of the world' (p. 29). Camus found within his own experience a 'divorce between the mind that desires and the world that disappoints': he suffers when he considers 'my nostalgia for unity, this fragmented universe and the contradiction that binds them together' (p. 44). Camus did not take the easy and popular path of denying the full reach of human longing so that we appear to fit neatly into the world. Rather, he faced what for him was an irreconcilable paradox. 'And these two certainties, my appetite for the absolute and for unity and the impossibility of reducing this world to a rational and reasonable principle, I also know that I cannot reconcile them' (pp. 45f.). Camus' experience was one of alienation: he felt imprisoned in a universe that had nothing in it immense enough to match the striving of the human person.

THE BLACK DEATH OF DEPERSONALISATION

In the Middle Ages people lived in terror of the plague: it was called the Black Death and was symbolised by a skeleton in a cowl with a vacant grin on the skull. In our day a new plague has laid waste to our civilization, the black death of depersonalisation. We have lost our sensitivity to the true quality and value of the human person and as a result we have begun to use one another and ourselves as instruments for our own pleasure and profit, or convenience, with no awareness of the damage this has inflicted both on the user and the used. Our death, too, has its symbol, the girl in the advertisement, the beautiful girl who adopts an undignified pose, and forces herself to wear an artificial smile and instrumentalise her sexuality in order to sell a commercial product. These depersonalised pictures are an inversion of the right relationship between products and persons. Properly, the product is an instrument which is meant to serve the person: in these advertisements the person is lowered to pretend that she is an instrument to sell the product. The pictures are also an inversion of the right relationship between sexuality and privacy. The proper context for sexual self-revelation is the privacy and intimacy of conjugal love: in the advertisement, sexuality is abused in order to seduce another person into buying a thing. The pictures also occasion depersonalised looking by those who see them. Those who pass by are invited to subject the image of a human person to disrespectful and instrumentalising looks. Every time we look in this way we are thereby depersonalised a little ourselves: our sensitivity to the mystery of the human person, to the extraordinary fact that beneath the human appearance there is a person-depth which is infinite, is blunted and distorted. These pictures constitute an ongoing conditioning and habituation that train us to find in the human body nothing more than the surface, and to ignore and quench any awareness that beneath this surface is a mystery of infinite preciousness. We look back in astonishment and disgust at our ancestors who owned and used slaves and never felt outraged that one person should be the property and tool of another. Our children's children will look back at us in pity and wonder how we could have been so closed to the humanity of the human person that we saw nothing wrong with making and displaying pictures in which a human person is stripped and made to pose and to fake happiness, like a slave at a Roman emperor's banquet, in order to sell commercial products. These depersonalised media excrements molest our senses day and night: they serve as a reminder of our enslavement to a false view of the human person; they are the fingerprint of the giant.

THE ILLUSION OF FAMILIARITY

The word familiarity reminds us of the family, the little community of husband and wife, of parents and children. They spend their lives very close to one another. They work hard to build up ways of intimate collaboration and cohabitation which respect the different temperaments of all the members and which leave room for everyone to blossom as a person. There is a great danger in family life of settling down like silt, of accepting ways of living together which are easier and more comfortable but which fail to respect some member of the family. There is an ever-present danger of settling into a bad habit of taking one another for granted. If this happens then the interlocking routines are nothing more than clever ways of avoiding the demands of respect for one another. The family is like a snake, it seems to die from time to time: but all that is happening is that it is shedding another skin. When this is about to occur, it means that one of the persons has come to a turning point, a growth point, in his or her life; usually it means that this person has discovered either a hitherto unnoticed knot which now demands to be untangled at once, or a new path of flowering which now demands to be followed. This is a testing time for the family as a whole, and for the other members. It is a typical human testing situation because it arises from the very nature of the human person as a being in whom there is a depth that is hidden to the eye. We should know that when we deal with human persons then this is one of the things that is going to happen from time to time. This eruption of a new dimension of one of the members can appear at first to shatter the family. But the family would not be a human institution at all if it could not adapt to these outbursts of person-growth. These apparent family explosions are not the death of the family but just a dramatic stage in its life. But because the person-depth is hidden from sight there is always the danger in a family that we can get into the bad habit of taking one another for granted: we can fall into the illusion of familiarity and treat one another, and ourselves, as if there were nothing more to each of us than the way of living, the temperament, the routines, that meet the eye at the moment. The illusion of familiarity is the forgetfulness of person-depth, the taking for granted of the people we meet as if they were finished products.

The illusion of familiarity can slip into our attitudes to people even more easily outside the family. We have all had the experience of being belittled by someone who squashes us into a mould that suits them: we have all felt the hurt of being demeaned by someone who misunderstands us. Familiarity can breed contempt, contempt for person-depth. We can allow ourselves to be tricked into thinking that we really know someone in depth when in reality we are only familiar with some of their superficial characteristics. The illusion of familiarity is our lack of sensitivity to the full reality of the people whose lives we touch. The illusion lies in the mistaken belief that just because we know someone's name, just because we recognise them, just because we see them with our eyes, we assume that we know them properly or fully. We are like snails who prefer to carry around all the time the shell of an inadequate routine, way of living or character instead of taking the trouble to smash these cramped shells and fashion a new routine, way of life or character more fitting of our person-depth. We are suffering from shell-shock: the illusion of familiarity stuns us into taking for granted that we are nothing more than what is expressed in our present routine. This shell-shock has become habitual and saps our energy. The inadequate view of the human being which dominates our society has deluded us into passively accepting the strait-jacket way of living which it imposes. A heavy sluggishness prevents us from undertaking a radical review of the way we understand the human person and the way we live. The false view of the human person leads us into a superficial and hollow form of social communication and interaction which is little more than the grating together of dead social shells. Does any of this ring true for you? Do you feel that the routines of your daily life provide opportunities for you to open and flower as a human person? Does the way you meet others and work together with them invite them to open and flower as persons? Do you feel that you are advancing in maturity and sensitivity as a human person from day to day? Or is the pearl of your personhood locked in a shell at the bottom of an uncharted depth?

THE SNAKEY PATH OF PERSON-GROWTH

If all this is really true, if each of us is a mystery, a being of infinite person-depth, then we are in serious trouble because the way we understand ourselves and the way we live denies, neglects, opposes and often violates what we are. And since we have lost most of our sensitivity to this dimension of our humanity we continue to inflict damage upon ourselves and one another unwittingly. It is a matter of the utmost urgency that we find out what we really are and change our ways of acting so that we stop hurting ourselves and other people. The first priority is to regain sensitivity, to regain consciousness of person-depth. But the path of person-growth is snakey in more ways than one. We have already mentioned the rhythm of death and rebirth which characterises the growth of the human person in the family: in the human person many passions and drives jostle for attention and our routine or way of life is only a temporary balance among them. As we learn more about them and about the right way to order them, we have to change the way we balance them and so we take on a new routine and way of life. These moments of important change appear often like deaths or breakdowns but in reality they are the stirrings of person-growth: they are like the sleep of death that falls on the snake while he is shedding an old skin and growing a new one. He looks as if he is dead but then he slithers off leaving behind his old skin. Our person-growth is marked by many such death-sleeps and skin-sheddings.

But our person-growth is snakey in another way also. The path we have to follow is not straight and clear but wriggly. Our quest for the lost secret of person-depth is not carried out alone. Each of us is a person among persons. For better or for worse they are our companions on the quest. And we cannot advance very far on the quest unless we change our attitude to these companions. We have become dead to our own and one another's personhood; we flatter and lie to get what we want. We manipulate others like puppets for our own purposes. We hurt them by using them as instruments or tools as if they had no ultimate value in themselves. When we begin to regain some degree of sensitivity to what it is to be a human being, to the mystery which each of us is, we feel a burning desire to change the way we treat other people, we feel the need to stop using others as if they were nothing more than implements for our convenience. To advance further on the journey to the Centre of the person we have to begin to lift the millstone of manipulation off our necks so that we can begin to breathe normally and act properly towards our fellow human beings. The routine habit of using people as our means hurts them. To be used in this way demeans and belittles people: it teaches them that they are nothing more than our tools. But this is not true: they are persons in their own right; so to treat them in this way is to deceive them about their own true value and immensity. By tampering with their humanity we teach them that such interference is an acceptable way to act towards human beings: this, again, is false: the inbuilt structure and fire of the human being is sacrosanct; so, to mess around with the humanity of a person is a gross act of immorality or, if the one who does it is so depersonalised that he or she is not aware of wrong-doing, a severe indication of personal disorder.

The routine habit of using people hurts the user also: when we use another as if he or she were nothing more than our instrument we violate not only their person-depth but also our own. In many cases they may be slightly better off because at least they have some suspicion that there is something wrong because they are being hurt, whereas we may induce in ourselves a convenient sincere ignorance of the damage we are inflicting on them. The routine habit of using people surrounds us with a shell of reinforced concrete which traps our person-depth within us and seals us off from the attempts of others to break through and liberate us.

It is for this reason that the journey to the Centre of the person has to follow a snakey path: where before we regarded ourselves as the only centre of the universe and barged straight towards whatever we wanted and trampled over whatever or whomever stood in our way, now, as we begin to regain sensitivity to person-depth in ourselves and others, we have to follow a more roundabout path. Now we begin to see that each person we meet is a shrine of person-depth, a centre of the universe. It is not enough to drive over them, we have to make room for each one in the appropriate manner. We have to be ready to stop and have a word or spend a moment with each one. We have to learn that most beautiful human pastime, listening to the story of another human being. We find that we are surrounded by living mysteries and we feel deep within us the call to pause for a heart-beat and to light a candle of respect before each one. There is a maze design on the floor of Chartres Cathedral which comes to mind when I think of the wriggly path of person-growth: it is a circular design and it seems at first as if you have only to walk straight in to reach the centre. But in fact the maze is so designed that you have to walk on every single line before you are led to the centre. When we begin to open ourselves to the full dimensions of the mystery of personhood we are led to follow the million detours of love on our way to the Centre of the person. Our task is the rediscovery and healing of our person-depth from the false way of treating one another which our society teaches. In this task we realise that our greatest help is the person nearest us: the neighbour is a great treasure because he or she can awaken in us a spark of person-depth and if we treat that person with due respect this spark is sheltered and fuelled and moves a step nearer becoming a viable flame. It may sound rather trite but a person's real riches are the people near at hand, because our most urgent task is to rediscover who we are and how we should live so as to open and unfold what we are; and in this task the person near at hand has a crucial role to play.

*The Myth of Sisyphus, Albert Camus. Translated by Justin O'Brien. (Hamish Hamilton, London, 1960)

EARTH LIGHT

1

Earth, you hide a passion in your heart
But the secret of your hidden fire is known
For sometimes the land is torn apart
And from the wound runs out the liquid stone.

2

An old face of the Earth,
Now from the heart estranged,
Gives way to a new, in birth:
The face of the Earth is changed.

3

Planet's blood with earth light incandescent
Congeals into a stone that floats:
Recalling the fire beneath ever-present
On which we sail the land like paper boats.

CHAPTER 2

THE LOST ALPHABET

DEPTH SOUNDING

We began with the question, Who am I? The real distinction between many external characteristics and myself led us to choose the word person to describe the kind of being each of us is, because that word hints at a 'more' which lies beneath the surface which those external aspects present. To reach this 'more' we changed the question into the form, Is there more to me than meets the eye? The human being, we found, has to be described as a mystery in the exact sense of that word, namely, a being in which there is a depth of meaning which as yet eludes us. This discovery faces us with a radical renewal of our attitude towards ourselves and other people. To describe this mysterious 'more' which lies beneath the surface of the human being we chose the word person-depth, and this enables us to redefine the task of human living in general and of the journey to the Centre of the person in particular, as the struggle to explore person-depth, to open and unfold it and to rebuild the surface of our lives so that it expresses and embodies ever more of the richness of the depth. This transformation of the surface by the riches of the depth which have been discovered and freed by exploration we have called person-growth. The present chapter continues the exploration of the question, How much more is there to me than meets the eye? In anticipation, we may keep in mind that all the talk of depth and surface is a picture, an image, a metaphor, to help us understand better, but at a later stage of the journey, in the next chapter, we shall have to abandon this imagery and face the hard question about what exactly this depth in us is.

For the moment, however, we stick to the question, How much more is there to me than meets the eye? What we want to know is,

How deep are we as human persons? We have spoken already about the presence in us of a depth which is infinite, of an infinite desire or capacity: how can we explore the depth of the human person? How can we measure the depth? What we want to do is depth sounding. We are familiar with adventure stories on film or television in which the crew of a submarine measure the depth of the sea by bouncing a sound off the sea-bed; it seems to be like radar. And as children we engaged in our own more primitive depth sounding by poking into a pool with a long stick or dropping a stone tied to a length of string into the water to measure its depth. How can we explore person-depth? What we need is something like a submarine or a diving bell, a bathysphere in which to explore our inner space: the craft in which we are going to carry out our deep self diving is the word. Our submarines are words, spoken or written. But our words have been wounded.

Just as we have become insensitive to the depth beneath the surface of each person, so we have lost our awareness of the depth which there should be in speaking and listening, in words, in communication. Language should provide us with a common perspective on reality and so unite us: but our language has been interfered with by powerful groups with vested interests. As a result our language has been to a great extent privatised. Many of the important words which should reveal to us the existence and contours of person-depth have been emptied of their proper meaning and filled with a superficial meaning. Commercial advertising in particular and the mass media popularisation of the many '-isms' and '-ologies' based on a denial of the depth in human beings have damaged our words so that they no longer function to put us in contact with the depth within us.

DEPTH-QUAKE

The vocabulary of the person has been damaged: the alphabet of person-depth and person-growth has been lost. Our words have been wounded and since we need them for the next stage of our journey to the Centre of the person, we have to pause and see how we can begin to heal them. We can start by asking about the original source of these words. The beautiful words which make up the vocabulary of the person were originally crafted to express experiences. This is the central point to be regained about words: they were made to express and communicate experiences. In order to understand a word properly we have to go back and find out what experience it was meant to express, then we have to undergo the same experience which led to the first uttering of that word. To understand a word we have to hold it up into the light of the experience which it was made to express. Words, then, have two sources: there is an original source in the first person who had a particular experience and created a special symbol to express it; and there are all the subsequent sources, namely, all the other people who are led by hearing or reading the word to undergo the same or a very similar experience and so to reach a position of being able to appreciate the real meaning of the word. Words, then, express experiences, people have experiences, so it is the experiences which people have that are the sources of the meanings of words.

We live in communities which last for many generations. The words formed by those who have special and significant experiences are handed down within these communities and the meaning of the words is passed on in the way of living that characterises the community. Like the communities, therefore, the words have a history, a memorable past, and part of the journey to the Centre of the person involves travelling in space and time to regain the lost memories and hidden histories of important words in the vocabulary of the person. But how do these important words originate? It is only when we have undergone an experience of exceptional intensity and intimacy that we are moved to go beyond the already established vocabulary and to carve out a new word to express the focal point of the new experience that just seized us. New words for the nature of the human person, and for the way we should live so as to open and flower as persons are born when our experience breaks out of the ordinary routine, when something from the person-depth below breaks through onto the surface. Often the new word is an already existing word which is taken and used in a new way to express what occurred in the new experience. Like the iron taken by the blacksmith which is heated in the fire and beaten into a new shape, so the old word is taken by the wordsmith and forged in the fire of the new experience so that it loses its old meaning and acquires a new function, namely, to articulate the new experience.

In us as in the earth, there is a depth beneath the surface. On the surface are our moods and attitudes, our likes and dislikes; like the earth's weather, these change continuously and quickly. Longerlasting than these are our settled routines, the ordered set of habits that makes up our character; like the earth's land surface these change only slowly and less obviously most of the time. But just as there is a fire beneath the surface of the earth so beneath the surface of our lives rages the heart's fire which strains and struggles for ever fuller expression above. The routines and character on the surface are only living as long as they are connected to this inner fire by open taproots. If this open connection between the fire at the heart and the routine and character on the surface is blocked or cut then our routine and character dry up and die and our heart aches with the suffering of enclosure and loneliness.

From time to time there occur massive upheavals deep within the earth which send shockwaves out from the centre to crack the surface and spew out the lethal lava that bears light. The human heart, too, from time to time, is awakened and stirs in its depth sending out depth-quakes which crack open and disrupt the settled routine and character of our day to day living. Such a depth-quake makes the tiny tasks of the daily round seem suddenly inconsequential for a while: it seizes our attention and by its intensity and intimacy imposes itself as the measure and standard of what we mean by fulfilment adequate to the human person. As the eruption of the earth's depth soon subsides and leaves behind lava congealed into a strange stone which serves to remind us of this exceptional experience and so of the fire beneath the ground, so too the depth-quake passes and leaves behind it words that have been transformed by its visit of fire. As the lava hardened into pumice-stone does not fully obey the ordinary rules of the surface — it floats in water — so too these new words, these old words which were drawn into the firestorm and transfigured so as to express the experience gained in that moment, do not fit in easily or completely with the rest of our vocabulary: and in that way they serve as a reminder that there is more to us than what is embodied in our present routine. The new words invite us to transfigure our present routine and character so that they embody more adequately what is implied by the glimpse of person-depth that occurred in the depth-quake.

FLOWERS OF FIRE

With winter and spring the cold and the warmth of spring sunlight awaken the seed that lies dead and hidden in the depth of the earth, it begins to grow towards the surface. The seedling breaks through the surface and grows towards the sun. In summertime the bush is ablaze with a fire of flowers. But the life of the bush does not end with the opening of the beautiful blooms. The flowers fade and wither and in their place light and brittle seedcases form. These detach from the bush and float away carrying the seed. These dry and delicate seedcases broadcast the seed. Many of them are lighter than air and sail around, like the helicopters of sycamore, the jinny-joes of dandelion, and the mollies of thistledown. I watched the children in the garden chasing them: I asked them what they called the fluffy things — 'Wishes.'

The centre of our humanity is a spark, a seed of fire. When it is awakened it begins to grow from the depth towards the surface of our lives. The seedling tears open the quiet clay of our daily routine and our accustomed character and grows into a burning bush blazing with flowers of fire. Among the flowers of fire are words. As flowers give way to seedcases that float away on the air, so the words formed to articulate the outbreak of the heart's fire cool and lighten, slip free from the context of the experience and drift away to become common property. Finders keepers. It is the nature of fire to spread: it is the nature of all life, too, to spread. And it is the nature of these special experiences of depth-quake not only to forge new words to express what is revealed in the experiences, but also to scatter these new words far and wide, to all and sundry, from the rooftop of the world. There is a risk in this, but life and fire thrive on this risk. It often happens that many of the seedcases end up in places where they cannot grow: but others land somewhere suitable and after a while a new life-cycle begins. And even seeds which fall into dry corners which offer no prospect for growth for years may at last be blown out of hiding into a crack in a path where there is just enough dust and damp to spark off the growth process. Words, too, often fall on deaf ears and lie low for centuries or even millennia without a chance to work their magic and open a new person to the depth within him or her; but then things can change, a new look can be taken at old dusty words, a new experience can awaken a half-forgotten memory of a once-heard, never-understood word, and the whole process begins again. A while ago in the news I heard about a family which found a brass cylinder on a picnic and had polished it up and kept it at home on their mantlepiece over the fire. Then they read a news item about someone who was hurt by an unexploded shell in the same area. They realised that their ornament was an unexploded shell! Our conversations are laced with many unexploded words just waiting to be set off by overhearing chance remarks about the mystery of the human person. How can we make these words speak to us? When an iron bar is held in very hot fire it becomes incandescent, it begins to radiate light: the words which reveal person-depth have to be held in the firestorm of person-quake; then they become incandescent with the meaning we seek.

DE-EDUCATION

Most of us have been processed through a state-monitored education system whose standards and content are largely determined by the state. This experience has damaged our ability to learn and our awareness of our need to grow as persons. For most of us education means going to school, doing state exams and memorising endless tracts of boring and irrelevant information which we flush down the pipe of oblivion as soon as we walk out of the exam hall. Our passage through the education system has taught us one lesson: learning and education are an arbitrary obstacle course with little or no bearing on our personal lives. This lesson is untrue but so horrible has been the experience of being put through the educational grinder that we have come out the other end completely turned off education. Never again, we feel. We have been conditioned by our education not to expect anything in education that is relevant to our personal flowering. We are packed with information but we know nothing about anything important to us as persons. We are victims of de-education. The word education comes from the Latin word *ducere* which means to lead, and the Latin suffix *e* which means out: so, education means to lead out from the student what is within him or her, in other words, it should centre around the discovery and opening of person-depth. Did your education do this? Was the principal topic on the courses the intimation of the richness of you as a human person and the indication of the well-tried paths of flowering by which this hidden treasure could be discovered, explored and unfolded in your personal life? Did this matter receive more attention than any other? It should have. If it did not, then is it any wonder that we find ourselves de-educated?

DEPTH-ILLITERACY

More people today can read and write, and so they have superficial

43

literacy. But the educational system has so damaged them that they do not expect to find in their reading and learning, anything of any relevance to their personal lives. Worse than this, they have been crammed full of useless facts but have never been invited and trained to descend into the depth of their lives to discover who they are and how they should live so as to flower. The illusion of familiarity has bewitched them in their attitude to words and education. They have heard or read all the right words: they are familiar with them: they think that nothing more is required for them to know the full meaning of the words. How wrong they are. They? We! When we read words which invite us to dive we miss the invitation. Our reading is superficial: we miss the depth. We are like someone drowning and reading a book on how to swim, who admires the beautiful style of the writer but never notices that he has anything to say about his predicament. The preponderance of closed views of the human person in the barrage of words flung at us by the media has programmed us to believe that there is no depth in the human person, that there is no urgent need to dive into this depth and explore it, and that there is no great personal benefit to be had from such an exercise. We are victims of depth-illiteracy. We no longer know how to speak about the depth; we have lost even very basic first steps in the vocabulary of the human person. We have lost the alphabet of person-depth and person-growth.

In economics there is a law called Gresham's law: it holds that bad money damages confidence in good money. In other words, if everyone knows that there are forged fivers about they will switch their money into singles until the forgeries are discovered and removed from circulation. A similar effect operates in the vocabulary of the person. Our speaking and listening, our reading and writing have been traumatised by the force-feeding with spiritual junk food to which we are subjected by the media. We are dazed by the devaluation of language brought about by chat-shows, disc-jockeys, non-stop entertainment, canned sentimental radio and television programmes and the gobbledygook of politicians. Newspapers, magazines, paperbacks and hardbacks pound into us the view of the human person ten times thinner than the very paper on which they are printed. Our television programmes have no true vision of the human person. Our radio programmes damage the tissue of person-depth more silently and unnoticedly than radioactivity damages our bodily tissue, numbing in this tissue any sensitivity to truth and depositing in its place a dead tissue of lies. If it is a crime to put poison in the public water-supply or to damage the currency by making imitation coins, then surely the corruption of our language must be among the more serious of the offences against the person?

COMMUNICATION - AN EXCHANGE OF WORDS?

The illusion of familiarity can mislead us into thinking that communication is nothing more than an exchange of words. All the more so when what we are trying to communicate concerns the hidden depth of the human person. Watered-down words and super-ficial entertainment have numbed us to the very existence of this inner depth. It is partly because we have lost the alphabet of person-depth that we are unable to recognise its presence within us. We need the alphabet of the person in order to establish internal communication between the depth and surface of our own life just as much as we need it to open communication with one another. We have discovered that words receive their meaning from the experiences which they are crafted to articulate. Now we have to ask what happens in communication.

What is it that we want to get across when we speak or write? We exchange words in order to share our meaning. But appearances can be deceptive. The mere fact of a successful exchange of words does not prove or guarantee that real communication has occurred. Do you recognise this experience? You pour your heart out to someone but their response shows that it has gone 'in one ear and out the other': you mutter that you might as well be talking to the wall. What, then, is the secret of real communication? How do we get our meaning across?

We have spoken of the woundedness of our words, the way in which they have been flattened and distorted by misuse. Now we have to notice that there is a trick involved in understanding this idea. The word, person, for example, looks and sounds the same whether it is being used by someone with a superficial understanding or by someone who understands it deeply. There is no apparent difference to the eye or to the ear. The illusion of familiarity deceives us into thinking that if we do not know the meaning of a word, then it has no meaning at all, or at least that it has no better meaning than the one we attach to it. The trick is to grasp that the wound is not really in the word at all, but in us. When I say that a particular word has no meaning for me I am pointing out a gap in my knowledge, a hole in my own head, not a defect in the word. The difficult point to grasp is, that a word is just a vibration in the air or a squiggle on paper. The meaning of the word is invisible, inaudible. This is the riddle of the sounds: a word sounds the same whether it is spoken by one with deep insight or by one who abuses the word for money. What kind of a thing is a word, then, if it sounds the same no matter how much meaning is in it? How can words look the same whether they have a little or a lot of meaning in them? What exactly is a word and how does it work? How do words carry meaning?

WHERE IS THE MEANING OF A BOOK?

Although we may seem to have strayed off the path of our original inquiry, this is not so. We have been trying to discover what exactly lies beneath the surface of the human life. We have seen that we need words to explore the depth and now we are examining how words work, how they mean. What we discover here is of the greatest significance for understanding person-depth and person-growth. We are coming at this point to a giant step in the journey to the Centre of the person. To go beyond the sound or the shape of the words we have to realise that their meaning is not really in them at all. The words are spoken or written by a person. But the words themselves do not understand or feel anything, they do not decide or communicate. The words are not intelligent. They were made by someone to express that person's meaning. To reach the meaning we have to go beyond the sound and the shape, even beyond what the familiar meaning of the words is, to reach what the person means.

To reach the meaning of the speaker it is not enough to see the words or to hear the words, even a cow could do that. We have to do more. We have to mind the words. We have to travel by means of the words into the mind of the person who spoke or wrote them, and to reach their meaning. Meaning is invisible: words do not contain meaning. But in some way they do something to us which enables us to reconstruct in our mind the meaning which was originally in the mind of the speaker or writer.

Let us take the example of a book. Where is the meaning of a book? Our instinctive reaction is to say, In the book, of course. Our imagination suggests the picture of the words containing meaning. The book is filled with meaning. The words carry the meaning across

46

from the speaker to the listener, from the writer to the reader. But the book does not understand the meaning it contains. It is just paper and ink stuck together with glue. Where is the meaning of a book? In the mind of the author: that much is sure. He wrote the book. But the author wrote the book and had it published in order to share his meaning with us. When is the meaning shared? When is the author satisfied? Would he be satisfied if millions of copies of the book were made but never distributed? Or if they were put on sale but never sold? Or if they were sold but never read? Or even if they were widely read but totally misunderstood? As far as sharing his meaning is concerned surely he will only be satisfied if what was in his mind is reconstructed in our minds? Only then will he have really communicated with us. Our work of minding his words rebuilds his meaning in our minds. The meaning, then, is first in the mind of the author: then when we have understood his words, it is in us. The book does not understand, so at no stage is there any meaning in the book.

Words, then are precision instruments, like a pair of spectacles. If we abuse a precision instrument we damage it and make it unable to perform its specialised function. If we see a nail sticking out of a doorway and try to hammer it back into the wood with our spectacles, we will break the lenses and the nail will still be left sticking out: we will have no glasses because they are now broken so we are likely to walk into the nail and hurt ourselves. Words are precision instruments for expressing experiences and for knowing parts of reality. If we abuse words then we will damage them and as a result we will be unable to express those experiences or to know those parts of reality.

Books, too, are precision instruments: they are a complex sign designed to move the reader to share the experience of the writer. Not just dry understanding, but feelings and decisions, changes in our life or in a whole society, can be precipitated by a book. Words and books, then, are mysteries: although they themselves contain no meaning they are able to spark off meaning in those who mind them. Words are like magician's hats: we look inside them and see that there is no meaning in them, but then, lo and behold, they produce meaning in us! They are like midwives; they have the art of bringing forth meaning in the mind of the beholder. An instrument can only be understood by examining not only the tool itself, but also the use which the maker and user makes of it and the effect which it produces. Words, and books, then, can be understood only by turning our attention to the way we make and use words and to the way in which words affect us.

WHY DO WE NEED SIGNS?

Words and books are signs. There is no meaning in a sign but it is so designed that it is able to spark off in others the same meaning that was in the mind and heart of the one who made it. It is not helpful to accept the picture which our imagination offers of the word or the book carrying or containing meaning. Picturing and imagining are not the same as understanding. Signs are things that are able to contact and affect our senses, things we can see or hear, taste or touch, smell or feel, or move. They are so constructed that they are able to move those whose senses they touch to generate experiences in themselves: on the basis of these they are moved to reconstruct in their minds and hearts the same meaning as was in the mind and heart of the one who made the signs. Some signs like those in mathematics are designed only to produce in us dry acts of understanding: others are made to move us to share emotions and decisions.

Why do we human persons need signs? Our need for signs has to do with the fact that we are mysteries. As well as the outer part which meets the eye there is an inner part which is invisible. If we are to communicate we need signs. The invisible part of me cannot get in touch with the invisible part of you without them. If you doubt this, then send me a message by telepathy and wait for my reply: but don't hold your breath. If you wish to communicate with me then you have to make something that can touch my senses, you have to send it to me, I have to be touched by it and moved to reconstruct in myself what you mean.

GOING BEYOND PICTURE-THINKING

This brings us to the end of the second stage of the journey, and points out the way which must be followed in the next stage. In the first stage we reflected on the presence of a depth beneath the surface of our living. We understood that each of us is a mystery, that there is in us a hidden meaning which we do not fully grasp and which is attractive to us. Next we began to ask how much more there is to me than meets the eye, how deep is the hidden depth within us. This led us to focus on words as the vessels in which we have to explore person-depth. We found that they, too, are mysteries, like magician's hats, empty and full at the same time. When we pushed this reflection we were led to conclude that it is only picture-thinking to speak of words carrying or containing meaning. We were thrown back once again to the persons who make and use words. The key to the meaning of words lies inside the persons who utter and respond to them. We are driven to the conclusion that there is in us a hidden part, an invisible dimension. Now we begin to see that all the talk of depth and surface has been picture-thinking. Now we have to face the difficult task of going beyond the pictures provided by imagination to explore what exactly is the invisible dimension within each human person.

EARTHLING

Take a star
Add some clay
In a thorough marling:
We are
Made this way
Earthling, Starling.

CHAPTER 3

JOURNEY TO THE CENTRE OF THE PERSON

THE CLIFF AND THE STORM

In a good adventure story there are always immense difficulties to be overcome, a swamp to be crossed, a desert, a jungle, an ocean or some other natural obstacle to be traversed. Often it is a great cliff that has to be scaled, and often at the height of a wild storm. Our journey to the Centre of the person has reached its cliff and there is a storm in progress. In the two earlier chapters the climb has been easier, the slope has been gentle. Now, however, the going gets more difficult. The cliff that lies ahead is the difficulty of leaving behind the imagery of depth and discovering what exactly we mean by it. The writing is more dry, and you have to check over and over again to discover whether what I say is an accurate account of what you find in your experience.

The storm that is raging about us as we try to scale the cliff is the war of words about what we are as human beings, a war between various '-isms' and '-ologies' which see people as nothing more than a part of nature, or a part of society. As a result of these squabbles, all the words which we have to describe the human person have already been given conflicting meanings, and we are likely to find in our own attitudes strong passions and prejudices that push us towards this and away from that meaning for a particular word. The storm, in other words, is inside us: we will probably find in ourselves many emotionally closed and aggressive feelings associated with some of the key words and ideas that we need to understand the nature of the human person. We will probably find in ourselves an unwillingness to face up to these wounds and undertake the work of healing them. We will probably feel like giving up the search and dodging the effort and suffering of regaining contact with our own humanity: after all, it would be so much easier to watch silly escapist programmes on the television or to go drinking and dancing with our friends. Well, you are free: if you decide you can stop reading or just read on without really engaging in the quest. You can turn back from the cliff and come in out of the storm. But above the storm and over the cliff . . .

We began with the question Who am I? A suspicion of those who tell us that we are nothing more than a part of nature or of society led us to transform the question into the form, Is there more to me than meets the eye? We described this 'more' as person-depth and its life as person-growth and we began to explore the possibility that the depth of the human person is not just great but in some sense infinite. This exploration is carried out through words, so attention was turned to the state of the words we use to describe the human person. The vocabulary of the person, we found, is damaged; the alphabet of person-depth is lost. As a first step in repairing and recovering the language of the human person we examined the way in which words work, how they carry or contain meaning. This helped us to focus on the presence in the human being of an invisible dimension. It is on this invisible dimension that we now concentrate, and to sharpen our focus we shall recast the question in the following form: What makes me more than an animal?

PLANTS

If we look at the world the first division that strikes us is between living and inanimate things. We clearly fall into the category of living beings. But what do we mean by living? Among living things, some are conscious and some are not; plants are alive but they are not conscious. Animals and human beings are alive and they are also conscious. To get a clearer understanding of what is meant by living compare a plant to a heap of sand. A heap of sand has many parts and they are close together, perhaps for many years. But the grains of sand have no set of relationships with one another such that these and only these parts go to make up this heap of sand. The relationships between the grains of sand in the heap can be explained in terms of the laws of physics and chemistry, and the same laws explain the relationships between the grains of sand and the surrounding physical environment.

A plant, on the other hand, is more than just an arbitrary part of the physical world: it is a distinct reality, characterised by a law unto itself. The many parts of the plant are definitely related to one another and to the whole plant according to an inner plan or order which directs the activities of the plant. The relationships between the parts and the whole ask to be understood as a pattern which governs all the activities of the plant in such a way that we grasp that it is a whole, a unity, which functions for its own inner purposes. Such a structured whole which acts according to an inner law is a living being. A plant is alive and its life is organic: it performs over and over again sets of movements and operations in which it extracts from the surrounding environment the materials that it requires to build itself up according to its inbuilt form, also it gets rid of materials that it does not use; it grows and matures and reproduces; and it adapts slowly to the environment.

In the case of the heap of sand, the relationships between the grains and the heap and between the heap and the surrounding world can be explained in terms of the laws of physics and chemistry: in the case of the plant, the relationships between the parts of the plant and the plant as a whole, while they obey the laws of physics and chemistry, also follow a higher set of laws, the laws of botany, in such a manner that we can grasp the distinct existence of the plant and distinguish it from the surrounding environment.

Just as we had to be on the watch out for a flattening of our sensitivity to the full reality of the human person by ideologies which say that a human being is nothing more than an animal, nothing more than a part of nature, so in the case of plants also we have to take care not to be misled into thinking that a plant is nothing more than a jumble of chemicals that happen to be stuck together. A plant is a mystery. If you find this difficult to accept, your sensitivity has been blunted. Are you willing to consider such a possibility? If we have lost some responsiveness to the mystery of plant life then we should try to retrieve it. We used the symbol of spring earlier in the journey: we may need to go back to this experience, to relive attentively the death of winter, the long wait when nothing seems to be happening and then the marvellous surge of new life that comes with spring. Our heart should feel the amazing quality of life. To be unmoved before the rebirth of spring is to be less than fully human.

But plant life is a mystery in a deeper way than that. It is not just a matter of cultivating an artificial wonder: the wonder is merited by the extraordinary kind of being that a plant is. Consider a plant at different stages of its life. At every stage it has a definite structure, for example, an acorn, a seedling, and a fully grown, mature oak tree. But from one period of its life to another the structure changes, so there is also an inner plan of unfolding that the changes follow. Unlike a house which is built according to a plan but by an external builder, the plant is self-operating, self-moving, self-assembling, self-developing. And most mysterious of all, the plant is a self-operator, a self-mover, a self-assembler, a self-developer. This is what is meant by alive, that it has within itself the principle of its own movement and operation, its own growth and development.

ANIMALS

In animals there is not only organic life but psychic or sensitive life. Animals have their own characteristic set of operations: perception, affection and aggression, imagination and memory, specialised bodily movements, interest and anticipation. Animals employ these sensitivities in the pursuit of strictly defined goals, nourishment, self-preservation, growth and reproduction. In animals, sensitive consciousness is specialised so that it responds to specific kinds of stimuli received through sight, hearing, taste, smell, touch and bodily movement and feeling from the external environment. The specialisation of animal sensitivity fits each type of animal to live in its own very narrowly defined external environment.

What we said about the mystery of plant life is true also for animal life. As there are operations and movements in plants which are not present in a heap of sand, and which require a higher set of laws to explain them, so there are operations and movements in animals which are not present in inorganic reality or in plants, and which require a higher set of laws, the laws of zoology, to explain them. And like the plant, the animal is a self-operating, self-assembling, self-developing whole which has within it its own principle of life.

When we move on now to try to understand and put into words the difference between animals and human persons we are not denying that there are areas of similarity between them, but we are trying to pin-point precisely the dividing line between them, the cliff that we mentioned at the start of this chapter. The question with which we began this chapter was, What makes me more than an animal? We can rephrase it, What is in me that is not in an animal?

The first word we have to use in the effort to understand more clearly what we mean when we speak of a depth in the human person is consciousness. This word has been used in different ways by different people but we shall try to give it a meaning that is tied to an experience which you can identify in your own experience. In a boxing match when one fighter is knocked out we say that he has lost consciousness. We are going to try to describe as carefully as possible what this consciousness is. The reason this is important is that we want to reach an understanding of the human person which is empirical and verifiable, in other words, we want to end up with something more than just another opinion: we want to reach something that is based on experience and which you or anyone else can verify if they wish by examining their own experience to discover whether what we say about the human person is accurate as an account of what they find in their own experience.

In each one of us there is a not-findable-by-the-senses part which we have called person-depth. What is it? It is my consciousness. But what is meant by consciousness? When I see a chair I am aware that I am seeing the chair. Is this true for you? Check it in your own experience. Look at a chair. Are you aware that you are seeing the chair? Look at the chair again. While you are looking at the chair your blood is moving through your veins in your arm but you are not aware of this movement. Are you? So, you perform actions which are conscious and others go on without your having to make any deliberate choice to start them and of which you are not aware. Is this true for you?

When I look at a chair the chair is present to me in and through the act of seeing. The chair is the object of my act of seeing and I am conscious of it as the object of my act. But I am also present to myself in the act of seeing the chair; I am aware that I am seeing the chair. I am present to myself in and through the act of seeing the chair. I am the subject of the act of seeing the chair and I am conscious of myself as the subject of my act. I am aware that I am looking. It is this self-awareness in the act of seeing that is meant when we call seeing a conscious act. An act is conscious when it has this self-presence as one of its properties. And as we have seen, I do other acts like growing my hair and nails which are not conscious acts.

Many of our actions have this self-awareness in them. Some of these are the actions which are similar to those of the animals like sensation and perception, affection and aggression, memory and imagination, interest and anticipation, bodily feelings and movements, the actions and passions we experience when we seek nourishment, self-preservation, growth and procreation. When we are hungry or thirsty, tired or afraid, angry or sad, attracted or revolted, we are aware of these experiences. The experience of pleasure or pain is conscious.

Beyond these actions and passions of sensitive or psychic consciousness we have other kinds of experience which are conscious: wonder, wanting to know, inquiry, questioning, playing with images, understanding, making suggestions, putting forward possibilities, grasping relationships and distinctions, expressing the content of insights in ideas and expressing these in words, all these are conscious; wanting to check and verify, drawing out implications, gathering evidence, presenting it and drawing conclusions from it by reasoning, working out conditions and checking whether they are fulfilled, reaching a judgement in a flash of understanding, expressing this in a statement and being moved by the being thereby known to an act of loving acceptance, all these acts are also conscious. When we work for a living, when we relax and enjoy entertainment, when we work artistically or creatively, when we play sports and engage in light conversation we are conscious. When we wonder what we ought to do, when we deliberate and evaluate, when we reach judgements of value, when we work out practically what has to be done and choose freely to do it, when we undertake responsibilities and keep our commitments and most of all when we build up lasting relationships of love and service with one another, we are conscious. So there is a wide range of human actions which are conscious in the sense that when we are doing them we are aware that we are doing them.

It is helpful at this stage to point out a danger so as to avoid it. When we try to understand anything our imagination rushes in to help by offering us pictures. As we saw in the case of words 'carrying' or 'containing' meaning, the pictures supplied so eagerly by imagination bring us some of the way towards understanding but at a certain point we have to leave imagination and its pictures behind and seek understanding. Now, when we try to understand what our consciousness is like, our imagination may throw up the picture of an inner look. Consciousness, it suggests, is like an inner look. When I see the chair, my consciousness of myself is like me taking an inner look at myself looking at the chair. We have to take care not to be misled by this image. Consciousness is not an inner seeing. Examine your experience again. When you see the chair there is only one act of seeing: you see the chair. There is no second inner act of seeing in which somehow you twist around inside yourself and catch a glimpse of yourself looking at the chair. That is just picture thinking. The facts of experience are that seeing just happens to be that kind of action which has self-awareness as a property: when I see something I am aware that I am seeing.

This enables us to make an important discovery. When we see a chair we are aware that we are seeing it but this awareness is not itself a second inner look. We do not see our consciousness: all we see is the chair. The consciousness is invisible! We have found at last the dimension of our being which is really invisible. The invisible part of me, or you, or any human person, the not-findable-by-the-senses part of each one, is consciousness. The consciousness of each human person is invisible not just in the sense that other persons cannot see it, but also in the sense that each of us cannot see his or her own consciousness: consciousness is just not the kind of reality that can be 'picked up' by eyes or ears or by any of the senses. Furthermore it has to be noticed that each one of us is only conscious of his or her own consciousness: none of us is able to tune in or to eavesdrop on the consciousness of another human person. We cannot enter the consciousness of another person as its subject, only as an object for it. Because of this empirical fact of distinct and private human consciousness we have to say that each human person is a unique entity and not merely a part of some imaginary or abstract whole made up of several people, like history, humanity or society: rather, although concrete, these wholes are secondary, accidental or relational unities made up by the coming together of human persons each of whom is really and truly a primary unity or whole, a distinct being in his or her own right. Society is for persons: from this it follows that there are definite limits to what society, or any other of these relational unities, may legitimately demand of the persons who participate in them. And these definite limits are derived from the nature of the human person. Society has no right to demand from the human person anything which would involve a violation of the inbuilt thrust of the human person.

Now that we have identified our consciousness as the reality intended by the symbol person-depth we can begin our exploration of it. A first observation is that we do not usually experience acts of seeing or hearing or tasting, or of the other senses, as occurring one at a time in complete isolation from one another. This is what I observe in my experience: is it what you observe in yours? Only you can answer that question and you can do so authentically only by directing your attention to your own experience of sensing. Do you just see red or feel hot? Or do these acts occur as already structured into perception in your experience? We discover by attentive concentration on our conscious experience that all the different kinds of conscious acts occur in our awareness already woven into a flow of awareness which is organised and has a direction and unity. Our acts of sensing are knitted together into a flow of perception. Our bodily experience and action in the world is a richly textured living tapestry in which acts like seeing and moving are bound up in the ongoing stream of our engagement in the world. Acts of hearing that noise or smelling that odour do not flash onto our awareness as static contents like slides on a screen: they occur already-dovetailed together like the pieces of a jigsaw puzzle, but a jigsaw puzzle with a moving picture, a living jigsaw.

We do not experience sensations in the same way that a viewer in a cinema watches the stream of sights pass before him on a screen: we are engaged in our surroundings by our interests and responses. Perception is the term for this fact of consciousness: our bodily acts like seeing and moving, feeling and balancing are present in our consciousness not as separate acts but as already structured into a flow of living experience.

We often speak of the third world. We mean that as well as the Eastern and Western blocs who seem to claim most of our attention, there is a poor part of the planet which is neither Eastern or Western. But there is only one world. The word, world, is being used in two senses. There is the one world which is the same for everyone, whether they know it or not: for example, the laws of physics apply just as much in India as in New York, and they do so whether or not the inhabitants know any physics. But we also speak of your world and my world and of failures and difficulties in communication that arise because people seem to live in different worlds. There is a real and important sense in which each one of us does live to some extent in a world of his or her own until we take steps to travel beyond it and enter a world common to others. This is due partly to the fact that our perception of the external world is structured by our interests, and as different individuals have different interests, so their worlds are different.

As an example consider the Mystery of the Purple Room. Several people enter a room with hideous purple wall-paper. Each one's perception is structured by his interests. One has just heard that he has only a month to live and is wracked by worry about how his family will survive financially after his death. The next person was in the room earlier and spilt tea on the carpet: he is consumed by anxiety in case his boss sees the stain and fires him over it. His eyes go straight for the blot and from there to the boss to check whether he has noticed it. The third person is a lover of rare shrubs: his eyes fasten on the plants in the corner: he spots a particularly desirable specimen. His passion is aroused. His fingers creep into his jacket pocket where he carries his special knife for just such occasions, for 'snatches'. All his actions in the room are directed to distracting everyone's attention from the shrub and slicing off a suitable portion of it while they are not looking. The boss's concern is to succeed in renting the room to the last man. He is fraught with distress and tension in case the client finds anything unsatisfactory about the room. He spots the tea-stain and anger and anxiety boil up inside him: he beams a malevolent glare at his employee which augurs ill for his future. The last man has chosen the room because with the right photographic equipment he should be able to get clear pictures of confidential documents on the desk of an important official whose office is visible from the window, across the street. Here we have seen several people all in the same room: but are they all undergoing the same experience? No. Their different concerns shape and determine what they experience. The plant-thief manages to get them all talking about a water-colour on the far wall while he ravages the unfortunate shrub. But although they all stand around looking and talking about the picture, their experiences are very different. The terminal patient is frantically doing arithmetic calculations in his mind: afterwards he remembers nothing of what was said or done. The boss is concerned to persuade the client that the room is just what he needs: he is only too eager to discuss the water-colour if it distracts attenntion from the tea-stain. The plant-thief has succeeded in getting a good cutting and he is already enjoying the story that the whole incident will make when he tells it later that evening to his fellow-enthusiasts at the pub. We have all had experiences like this and we are all familiar with the difficulties which this fact of living in different worlds creates for ordinary communication. Take any day at home: the son is upset because he has been in trouble at school over a copied exercise; the daughter is trying to watch her favourite programme on the television; the mother is at a crucial stage in a pavlova; the father is trying to remember where he put the rake. We really do live to some extent in different worlds.

Although it is true that we do live partly in different worlds, it does not follow that we cannot communicate with one another, or that we have to stay in those separate worlds. What are required are journeys to other worlds. We have to learn the secret of travel between worlds: how do we leave the partly closed world of our own interests and concerns and cross into the other world of another person's interests and concerns? This travel between worlds is an important part of the journey to the Centre of the person in which we are engaged. How do we begin to learn the art of journeying to other worlds?

In our own contemporary efforts to leave our planet and venture into space, a necessary first step before journeying to other outer worlds, the main problem to be overcome is gravity. The space-craft has to build up enough force in the upwards direction to over-ride the downwards pull of gravity. Our present problem of getting beyond the world of our own perceptions and interests and entering wider worlds common to many, has an analogous problem to that of reaching physical lift-off. How do we begin to go beyond the enclosing and limiting circle of our own interests and perceptions? A start in the search for an answer to this question is had by considering the partial independence and play of our imagination and memory.

THE PARTLY INDEPENDENT PLAY OF IMAGINATION AND MEMORY

Compared with the outer senses like sight and touch, memory and imagination have a partial independence from external stimuli and causes. I am in the dark. Suddenly a light flashes. This causes in me an act of seeing. The object and cause of my act of seeing is the light flashing: the subject of my act of seeing is me. I do the seeing. But not all of me does the seeing. Not all of me is able to see. My hair and feet do not see the flashing light: my eyes do. To express this specialisation we may say that the eye is the organ of sight: it has the power or capacity, the faculty or ability, the potentiality, to see. The external act of the light flashing causes the internal act of my eye, the act of seeing. Of course my eyes do not work by themselves: the brain and the nervous system play a part: to be accurate we have to say that it is I, the human being as a whole, who see, through or with my eyes. The point I want you to notice is the high degree of dependence of the eye and its act of seeing on the external stimulus: an internal act of seeing occurs because an external act of flashing occurs; unless some external act of burning or radiating occurs, internal acts of seeing do not occur.

When I consider a similar instance in the case of the imagination and memory the degree of dependence is less. I imagine now what is not present to my senses, for example, my sister. Or I remember a meal I had with her last month. As in the case of the act of seeing, I am the subject of the act of imagining or remembering. But it is not at all as easy to say what is the object of this act. Nor can we as clearly point to the external cause of this act. In a sense, my sister is the cause and the stimulus: but only in a sense, because it is more accurate to say that she was originally the cause or stimulus on which the image or memory is based. But it is the image or memory itself which is the object of the act of imagining or remembering.

We are able to explore these problems because imagining and remembering are conscious activities: when we imagine or remember, we are aware that we are imagining and remembering. So we can begin to explore them more deeply by asking questions about them. The flashing light was the object of the act of seeing: what is the object of the act of imagining and remembering? My eye was the specialised organ through which I did the act of seeing: what is the specialised organ through which I do the act of imagining and remembering?

As before, when we ask questions, our imagination tends to rush in with images to help us understand: so in this case, our imagination tends to come up with the answer, the brain! Surely we imagine and remember with the brain? Let us consider this suggestion: is my imagination *in* my brain? We have to say, yes and no; in other words, it depends what is meant by *in*. If we examine the way experts who study brains speak about this matter, we have to qualify and refine the statement that imagination and memory are *in* the brain. What experts in the study of the brain find in the brain is not imagination and memory, but the physiological foundation for imagination and memory. If they had nothing to go on but the brain itself, they would have no reason to conclude to the existence of the power of memory or imagination. In fact they combine what they learn from the study of the brain with what they learn about imagination and memory from the study of people's descriptions of how their imagination and memory operate. And they draw conclusions in the form, such and such a disorder of memory is reported by people who are found to have such and such an observable damage to the brain.

The study of the bodily organ, the brain, does not discover the imagination and the memory; it discovers what it understands to be the bodily foundation of imagination and memory. What data has to be studied to discover imagination and memory directly? The data of conscious experience. To be precise, then, we have to say that imagination and memory are *in* consciousness.

When something is present in front of us in broad daylight, as soon as we open our eyes we see it. Our eyes are bound to see what lies before them. The same cannot be said for our imagination and memory. They are not bound by the same necessity and dependence to the physical things that touch the external senses. True, they get their original material from these senses or from consciousness but then they can store it and bring it out of storage, and they can move it around in a manner that is partly independent of the original external causes. For example, I have a row with my boss. On the way home that evening I re-run the row in my imagination, using some of what actually happened which I remember. But I change it all around. I tell the boss a few home truths, which somehow or other, I never got around to mentioning during the row. I think up a brilliant answer to what he said, which unfortunately never crossed my mind at the time. Have you not had this experience of re-arranging in a new way in your imagination bits and pieces drawn originally from experience, but now stored, recalled, moved about and altered in ways that they never were in experience? This is what I mean when I say that the imagination and memory are partly independent of the external senses.

The next characteristic of imagination and memory which we have to notice is the way they are able to help different interests and drives in us at different times. Our imagination is not tied to any one biological function: it is able to assist hunger, fear, anger or any of the other passions that we have in common with the higher animals. For example, I remember that during a pilgrimage on which we had to fast, we found ourselves thinking and talking incessantly about food. Neither, however, is our imagination tied to helping only the biological functions: it plays with images also when other, strictly human interests have taken hold of us. When we are gardening or decorating, building a model aeroplane or looking for something we have lost about the home, our imagination lends a hand by throwing up for us images that might be useful. My son brought a broken digital watch in to me the other day. He was convinced that the battery was in upsidedown. He had managed to take the back off the watch. Now he wanted to unscrew the cover that protected the batteries. The screws were too small for our smallest screw-driver. He asked me to help. After the five-hundredth request I resignedly agreed to try. I tried the smallest screw-driver and had to agree with him that it was too big. As I stared blankly at the wretched watch a niggling memory prodded its way into my imagination. I tried to focus on it but that did not work. I vaguely remembered something relevant to this problem. What was it? I could not remember. Then, like a bolt from the blue it arrived out of my memory and into my imagination. Some time previously I had opened some similar tiny mechanism, now what was it? I could not recall what it was that I had opened. But then suddenly it was there in my imagination, the kitchen knife, the little black one: the point of that knife was the edge that had been thin enough the last time. Are you familiar with this operation of imagination? The way we are able to want a particular image or memory, and without being fully or consciously able to direct its activity, we set off a search in which, sometimes, just the right memory or image is extracted from wherever it is they are all stored? Both of these functions are amazing, the storage and the retrieval when required: and neither are fully under our conscious control. We can strain and want for all we are worth and get nothing, and yet sometimes as soon as we relax out pops just the image we wanted. Our imagination and memory are like that, partly under our direction and command, but only partly.

The most significant aspect of imagination from our viewpoint here is its ability to free the image from its perceptual origin and to play around with it under the direction of different human drives. As an example of this playing with images I remember trying to write a poem. As a teenager I used to walk very often along the West pier in Dun Laoghaire and around Seapoint. The poem was what I would now call an exploration of my experience of the search for the meaning of human existence and in particular for the meaning of love and evil. It was named Gull. This was a symbol drawn from my many experiences of watching the gulls and listening to them. So here was a first perceptual origin, the numerous, largely forgotten occasions on which I saw and heard seagulls. But I selected the seagull for several reasons. Firstly, because the cry of the seagull sounds sometimes like a cry and sometimes like a laugh: so it seemed or felt appropriate to express the double theme of love and suffering related to evil. Again, the word gull itself has resonances that also intimated these themes; it sounded like *gol* the Irish word for crying, and girl, to symbolise love. Furthermore, the flight of the birds had moved me many, many times, and awakened in me a thirst for transcendence. Again, the birds in the distance as they flew seemed to resemble the letters M and W which struck me as suitable images of man and woman, thus enriching the pool of associations that could be drawn on to express the themes of love and suffering as related to the achievement of transcendence. In this example, the free play of imagination is evident: images drawn from many different times and places, from different areas of my experience, are juggled about in and by my imagination, and by the very forces in me which the poem was to articulate, love, suffering, the quest for the meaning of life and the drive towards transcendence. Through these symbols, those forces which at that time were unnamed, could find an initial expression and exploration. And to take a related example: I was often impressed by the way other kinds of birds sometimes fly as a group, like a school of fish, so that when some turn, the group seems to wheel with them. I remember one evening while I was washing up the dishes being struck by the resemblance between the way the tea-leaves swirled as they went down the drain, and the swerving movement of the birds, and I remember making a mental note of the image as a possible part for a poem. Here again, the point is that the images began as perceptual but are then freed once they are inside the imagination, and that when another interest takes hold of the person, in this case an artistic interest, the images can be summoned back, or may just arrive back unsummoned, but in a form disengaged from the original perceptual context. A final example, again of my artistic bird-watching. During a stroll I was struck by the sight of several birds sitting along a set of telephone wires between two poles. It sparked off in my imagination a likeness or comparison: they were like notes of music on a sheet of scoring paper. I give these to illustrate the fact that the images which come to us in a particular perceptual context are then freed in and by the imagination and move about partly in answer to direct commands from other drives and concerns in us, and partly about their own business, which often springs surprises on us by producing just the right image or memory when we had stopped trying to summon it.

GOING BEYOND ONESIDEDNESS

We are arriving now at the most important and difficult part of the journey to the Centre of the person. I am hoping that you will work your way through the following sections and arrive through them at a spark of understanding of what you are as a human person. If you meditate on them for a while I hope to communicate to you some understanding of the nature of the human spirit. The rest of the journey hangs upon what you discover about yourself from the following sections.

The question that is guiding us during this stage of the quest is, What makes me more than an animal? What is it that is in me but not in any animal? We began by describing what we have in common with other beings. We gave a brief description of this kind of consciousness, sensitive consciousness. It is characterised in us by senses of sight, hearing, touch, taste and smell, by perception, memory and imagination, bodily movement and in various bodily drives and passions related to the bodily objectives of maintenance, growth and generation. Thus far, then, we have concentrated upon what we have in common with the higher animals. Now we begin to move on to ask where we differ from them. Why do I say that I am not an animal? What is it that I find within me that differentiates me from the animals?

At the beginning of this chapter the images of the cliff and the storm were introduced. The cliff symbolises the discontinuous jump that faces us, nay, that strikes us in the face, when we turn from animals to human beings. The storm symbolises the modern confusion and conflict about the relationship between man and the animals, the dispute about the nature of the human being. The view which is dominant among the social elites which control the institutions of education, east and west, sees man as an animal. Instead of a sheer cliff, they see a gradual slope: human beings are animals of a more advanced, developed or evolved type. They arrive at this conclusion because they examine only one side of the data, the outside. They study the bodily appearance, structure and function of animals and human beings and they conclude that because human beings and animals have similar bodily appearances, structures and functions, it follows that human beings are nothing more than another species of animals, although they may say we are the highest type, so far!

However, such an approach disqualifies itself from being admitted as scientific precisely because of the refusal to examine the other side of the data, the inside. The difference that separates human beings irrevocably from the animals is to be found on the inside, in other words, in our consciousness, that invisible, inner part of us that makes us a mystery. We have to go beyond this onesidedness now and to move from the outside of the human person to the inside.

KNOWING

KNOWING IS NOT LIKE LOOKING

We have already come across picture-thinking, the tendency of the imagination to throw up pictures to help us understand things. When we ask what knowing is we meet it again: our imagination comes up with the suggestion that knowing is like looking. Knowing, we imagine, must be like taking a look at something that is there in front of our inner eye. This is no more than an image and to understand what we are as human persons we have to leave the rich jungle of imagery and venture out into the desert, the dry region of clear and accurate analysis, in which, instead of letting images direct our inquiry, we turn our attention to what we actually do when we know something. We need to go out into this desert, if for no other reason than to throw sand into our eyes, and so subvert the powerful hold which this misleading image of knowing as a kind of inner look, has over us.

Whenever I hear people speaking about knowing as if it were like looking I remind myself of François Huber. He was born in Geneva in 1750. He became interested in the study of bees and dedicated his life to this work. When he was young, however, he went blind! Despite this handicap, with the help of his assistant, Burnens, he spent his whole life in the study of bees. In 1789 he wrote the first volume of *New Observations on Bees* in which he reported some of his discoveries, and the second volume containing others was published twenty years later. Many multitudes of people had looked at bees day after day throughout their lives and had understood little: here was a man who could not see them, but who understood more than all these others. He is a testament to the fact that knowing is not taking a look.

DO IT YOURSELF!

The best way for you to travel this stage of the journey is to do a bit of new knowing and to pay attention to what you are doing while you are knowing: this will put you in a position to check whether what I say is an accurate account of what goes on in you when you know.

Human knowing, as we shall discover, is not a single act like a look, but a process with a definite structure. It is made up of different parts which fit together in a particular way. Our knowing has parts. These parts are conscious activities. They are not all the same kind of act, but different kinds of act which combine together in a particular order to constitute a piece of human knowing. No one of these kinds of act, taken by itself, and apart from its place in the process as a whole, is human knowing: it is just this or that part of it.

Some of the conscious activities which go to make up knowing are acts of sensitive consciousness: seeing, hearing, tasting, smelling, touching, remembering, imagining, feeling and moving. Others are activities found only in human beings: inquiring, asking questions, understanding, expressing in concepts and words, wanting to verify, working out conditions, checking whether conditions are fulfilled, judging and expressing this in judgements or propositions. To present the nature of human knowing I am going to try to describe what I do when I am doing a crossword puzzle. This kind of exercise involves several bits of knowing and gives us an opportunity to notice and point out the more important features in human knowing.

While you are working through the following part, the important question is not What is the right answer to the clue? but How am I going about answering the question? What am I doing as I try to know? The more difficulty you have in getting the right answer the better, because then you are more likely to notice yourself doing the various activities that are involved. If you cannot do crosswords or find this one too easy, then find something more suitable or difficult and use that.

Across.
1. A number of fingers. (5)
2. J.A.S.O.N. — (8)

Down.
3. A strange drink. (3)
4. HIJKLMNO (5)

Keep in mind, then, that your main focus of attention has to be on what you are doing while you are trying to work out the answers, rather than on the puzzle itself. In what follows I shall partly describe what I do and partly ask you whether you are doing the same kind of thing. What, then, is the first thing you are doing to do the crossword puzzle? Are you looking at the page? Here is a starting point for human knowing: I experience something; something touches my senses in some way and I become aware of it. My knowing is always knowing something, something that I experience. I begin from experience. Perhaps the clearest way to present the account of knowing is to make a list of the parts as they occur.

The work that follows is meant to be empirical; that is, I mean that if you want to, you can do what is proposed and by studying what you experience as happening in your own consciousness, discover whether what I am suggesting is a correct account of what you do when you are knowing. You can verify my account in your experience. We may call what we are doing here Performance Analysis: I am doing a piece of knowing and trying to understand at the same time what I am doing when I am performing that act of knowing; and I invite you to do the same. It is an analysis of one's own performance of knowing.

1. *Experience.*
What is the first step you perform in your attempt to do the crossword puzzle? What sets off the very attempt to do it in the first place? For me it is seeing the crossword puzzle and the clues on the page. Before I saw them I was not interested in doing it: the sight of them awakened in me an interest in the puzzle. This, then, is my first discovery about the way I know: it begins from something that I see,

or sense, or experience in some way. An experience provides what we may call the data on which the subsequent piece of knowing works or builds. Whenever I know, it is always a case of my knowing something, and the basis of that knowing is something that I experience. Is this the case for you?

2. *Inquiry.*

As I look at the clues and the diagram I notice that my looking begins to concentrate or to focus. I am not allowing my gaze to wander at random all over the page or the room: no; I start to pay particular attention to a special set of data, the clues and the crossword boxes. Do you notice this fixing of your gaze on the data, on one area of your experience? Are you aware that you are zoning in on the clues and the boxes rather than on the noise of traffic, or birds, or other people, nearby?

I notice that at the same time I am becoming interested in the puzzle. I experience not only the change from staring about or looking to studying the puzzle, but also the starting up of a new interest. And what is this new concern? I find that it is a desire to work out the right answers. I am becoming interested in the puzzle: I want to know the right answers. I want to work out what words fit into the boxes and correspond to the clues. I am beginning to inquire, to wonder, to study, to want to know. I read the clues carefully, intently, with concentration. This is experienced as a heightening of attentiveness. Do you notice in yourself this beginning of inquiry? Does the sight of the puzzle awaken in you a desire to know the answers?

Animals may see crossword puzzles. But never in the whole history of humankind has it been recorded that a cow or a parrot took up its pencil, licked it, and began to work out the answers. Why not? Because there is something in us that enables us to wonder and inquire and that makes us want to know the answers: and that something is not in the animals. I never cease to be amazed at the way our children ask questions about everything under the sun, and even about things not under the sun (Daddy! What is outside space? — Oh, eh, well, why don't you run along and play now.) I notice that this interest or desire, the wanting to know, the wonder, the inquiry, soon erupts into questions. Do you notice this? It might help if you got a few people together to try to do the puzzle and even more importantly, to try to express out loud what they are doing as they try to do the puzzle. I read the first clue across. 1. A number of fingers. (5). I think to myself: I wonder what he is looking for. What does he want? Is it a figure? What numbers have five letters? Spontaneously, I ask questions. They are about the data that is given in my experience. I look at the clues and the boxes and I ask What would fit in here? Inquiry bursts into questioning. To make it clearer we can say that at this stage the typical kind of question is of the form, What is this? In this what-questioning I am trying to find the "what" that relates the clue and the spaces in the box.

It is important to notice at this point that this "what" is invisible. I cannot see with my eyes the answer to the first clue. I can stare at it until the cows come home but looking with my eyes does not bring the answer. I am searching for something that cannot be seen with the eyes. And I am carrying out this search with an invisible part of me. My inquiring desire to know cannot be seen with the eyes either: it is present to me because it is a conscious act; but in no sense can I be said to see it. So a not-findable-by-the-senses part of me is seeking a not-findable-by-the-senses part of the puzzle. And this seeking proceeds by inquiry, wonder, desiring to know which breaks out into questions, what-questions about experience. Do you notice this occurrence of questioning?

3. *Playing with images.*

When my interest intensifies and brings about the zoning in of my looking on the data, the clues and the boxes, I notice that I begin to straighten up the page and move it about so that I can see the clues and the boxes properly and clearly. If I am working from a newspaper I fold it so that I can get at the puzzle easily. I settle down to it. I turn the page around so that the light falls on the puzzle. Then I focus on the clues and the spaces. If it is, for instance, an anagram, I usually find that I have got a pencil and have begun to try out various arrangements of the letters in the margin of the page. Do you notice in your approach, the spontaneous tendency to do something like this? Again, when I have filled in several of the clues and am left with a few letters at the end of a word, for example -ock, I notice that I spontaneously begin to remember and run through lists of words that have that ending in my imagination. Clock, knock, block, rock and so on. This is playing with images. Inquiry, the desire to know, leads me to play around with the images. It leads me to disengage images from the purely perceptual experience offered by the page with the clues and the crossword boxes. I begin with what is experienced on the page: but soon I am working with the more flexible and plastic images that I make and move about in my imagination. I notice that I close my eyes or stare at nothing in particular, while in my imagination I am wondering ". . . a number of fingers, five fingers on a hand, ten fingers altogether, one, two, three, four, five, six, seven, eight, nine, ten . . ." Do you notice this free play of imagination under the influence of the desire to know starting from what is given in experience, but not staying with that, rather, letting that spark off images and associations, memories and pictures?

4. *Understanding.*
Suddenly, while I am playing with the images and trying to understand the clues, I get a flash of insight: "Aha!" It is a bright, uplifting, happy moment. The tension that the inquiry had built up in me is released. This is a delicate stage in our journey because that simple little act of insight is one of the key happenings in the whole vision of the human person that we are exploring and trying to share. It is such a quick visitor that it is easy to miss it. In fact it is so bound up in the inquiry and playing with images that come before it, and with the spontaneous articulation of its content in ideas and concepts that comes after it, that we very easily neglect it and thereby fail to notice its extraordinary qualities and nature. So, we have to take care not to pass over this tiny explosion of understanding. When I feel "Aha! I've got it!" I immediately rush ahead to utter in ideas and concepts what it is that I have 'got': and by studying this uttering in ideas and concepts, we will get a better understanding of what exactly has happened in this little explosion.

5. *The expression of what is understood in ideas, concepts and words.*
Go back, for a moment, to the flow of images that came into my imagination while I was puzzling over the first clue. The data were the words 1. A number of fingers. (5). The flow of images was ". . . a number of fingers, five fingers on a hand, ten fingers altogether, one, two, three, four, five, six, seven, eight, nine, ten . . ." At this point I remember a flash of understanding. "Aha!" Immediately after this little outburst of insight, out tumbled the ideas and concepts and words which express what it was that I had understood. "Leave out the thumbs and there are eight fingers: E, I, G, H, T, that has five letters!" Do you notice in yourself this order of events: inquiry into

data given in experience leads to playing with images; then insight emerges out of this play with the images in the imagination; and immediately after this, the mind utters for itself the content that it has just grasped in the flash of insight? Notice that we do not have to stop and wait until we reach a decision to go ahead and conceptualise the content of insight: on the contrary, no sooner has the explosion of understanding occurred than we spontaneously turn from the concentration on the image to the expression of what it was that we have grasped in the insight.

Notice also that we leave some of the image and even more of the data experienced behind us when we have the insight. Spontaneously we ignore the colour of the paper, the type of print, the year and month and day, the weight of the paper on which the clue is printed, the colour and thickness of the ink in which the letters of the clue are formed, and the full stops after the number 1 and the words of the clue, as well as the brackets around the number 5. These are not relevant and we know it. We know that the insight would be the same even if we had been doing the puzzle out in the garden instead of in the dining room. The insight also leaves behind the image which prompted it: is it not the case that the insight is not the same as the image? Do you notice in yourself the distinction between the flow of images and the supervening "Aha!" which they set off in you? Are these identical? I find that they are two different kinds of act altogether: the first is a flow of images in the imagination; the second is a grasp of an arrangement or relationship which is why the bits in the image and in the clue are the way they are. And the procession of ideas and concepts and words in which this arrangement is expressed or uttered is another act again. The insight itself was pre-verbal and even pre-conceptual. It was just a sheer grasp of a relationship, a connection, an order, a pattern. The conceptualisation abstracts from the data and the image just what is essential to the insight and generalises that. Thus, when I have the insight that 'eight' might be the right answer, I spontaneously leave out the fingers part of it: a picture of fingers is not part of the answer or part of the utterance that spills out in my mind.

We said that the examination of the act of conceptualisation would help us to clarify what had happened in the preceding act, the little outburst of insight. Now we can appreciate that while the flow of images was, in a sense, playing around with the original experienced data, the act of insight is the grasp of a relationship that could account for the various bits of the data being the way they are. If eight is the answer, then that explains two things; firstly, it accounts for the number five between the brackets, for there are five letters in the number eight; secondly, it accounts for the phrase 'A number of fingers', in the clue, because on my two hands there are eight fingers, excluding my thumbs.

6. *Wanting to verify.*

No sooner have I had the insight and expressed what it had grasped than a new experience begins in me: I start wanting to verify the insight. This is a new level of inquiry, a sort of second stage. Do you notice how this further kind of desire to know commences once you have had an idea? I find that my mind is not satisfied by just any idea, it wants to go on to discover whether that idea is the correct one. This new inquiry also bursts into questions; do you notice in yourself this emergence of is-questioning? Eight *could be* right: but *is* it? Does it fit in with the other clues? It appears to answer the clue and to have the right number of letters, but is it really right? It is possible, but is it the actual answer? The awakening of this new level of inquiry directed not only to the original data, but now also to the new idea, makes us see the idea as a possibility, and only a possibility. It could be, but is it? Furthermore, the new level of inquiry shows that I am not satisfied with mere possibility: what I want is reality. Not what might be or could be, but what *is*, what really and actually is the right answer. And with the underlining of that little word 'is' in the last sentence we come to another key moment in our journey. For the moment let us just say that already we have noticed in the spontaneous drive of the desire to know, a desire to go beyond what is possible or what merely appears, to reach what *is*.

How do I go about checking whether my idea is correct? I find that I spontaneously return to the data: I go back to the crossword puzzle and the clues. I begin to examine the data again, but this time my question is different. Now I am asking, Does eight fit in with anything else? Does it fit all the facts? Does it fit in with all the relevant facts? Does it leave anything out? Does it fail to take anything into consideration? These are all what we have called is-questioning. At once, again, spontaneously, my imagination begins to play around with the images. I notice that I am running through the numbers from one to ten again in my imagination, this time quickly checking how many letters there are in the numbers. I arrive at seven and find myself counting out S,E,V,E,N, on my fingers. Five letters. A problem! If eight and seven both have five letters, then why should eight be the right answer: why not seven? I look at the boxes and notice that the spaces and boxes for Three Down begin at the second letter of One Across. If I could discover what Three Down is, then its first letter would be the second letter in One Across and that would tell me which of my two possibilities was correct. Do you notice the awakening in yourself of this second level of inquiry, the desire to verify?

7. Working out the conditions.

As we can see already from the last paragraph, the desire to verify leads us to reasoning. If this fits, then that should be the same across as well as down. What am I doing when I am reasoning like this? For a start, I am concentrating once again on the data and playing around with images. I am asking whether I have taken all the aspects into consideration and whether I have left anything out. Now I begin to reason with ifs. What is happening here? I have come up with two insights. Eight, and now, seven. Both have five letters. Which is right? Spontaneously I begin to work out what conditions would have to be fulfilled in order for me to be able to ascertain which possibility is correct. I am led by this line of inquiry to turn again to the data. I notice a little word-box leading down from the second letter-space of One Across. I understand that if that word begins with i, then eight is correct, and if it begins with e, then seven is the right answer. Do you notice yourself performing this action, working out what conditions would have to be fulfilled in order that a possibility might be verified?

Next, I find myself studying Three Down. I begin with the data given in experience. 3. A strange drink. (3). I think, "Well, it should be easy: after all, it only has three letters." An image springs into my imagination, a bottle and a spoon. Cod liver oil. An insight. Oil! Hardly. A strange drink. In three letters. Suddenly, an insight. Rum. At once, the process of verification races ahead. I should mention here, that such easy examples are little use for distinguishing the various parts of our knowing, because whatever we have already understood is retrieved by us more or less easily without having to go through the work of struggling to understand it all over again. It becomes habitual in us and as soon as it becomes relevant, more or less, we activate it again. For example, you are not thinking, at this

74

moment about the Latin for eight or the Roman god of war, but if I ask you where the names of the months came from, you can reactivate these insights fairly easily.

Three Down is an easy clue. A strange drink, in three letters. Rum fits because rum is a drink and also means strange. It is likely to be correct because it accounts for so much of the relevant data: it has three letters, it is a drink, and it means strange. I cautiously jot it down in pencil, lightly. I notice another problem. If rum is correct then eight and seven are in trouble! At once my imagination runs ahead seeking a number whose second letter is r. A dead end. I turn to the rest of the puzzle, the other two clues. Do you notice in yourself such a manner of attacking the problems?

8. *Working out whether the conditions are fulfilled.*
Already we have raced ahead to the next stage. As soon as we had worked out what conditions would have to be fulfilled in order that this answer be correct, we proceeded to work out whether in fact these conditions are fulfilled. This is what we did with the two possible answers, seven and eight. If seven was correct, then Three Down must begin with e: if eight was correct, then it must begin with i. That was the condition. Was it fulfilled? The drive to answer that question led to a renewed attention to the data. Here we have to distinguish two steps: working out what the conditions are, and working out whether they are fulfilled. Are they identical? If not then they are distinct.

At this point, it is worth noting another aspect of our knowing. We do not work at such a slow and simplified rate that it is easy to separate out as clearly as we are doing here, the various parts of knowing, straight away: in fact, we race through several parts very fast and it is only when we get stuck at a particular stage that we have a chance to study the elements of knowing which are involved at that point. So the example I am working through here is stylised to speed up the presentation. If you want to go into the structure of human knowing in depth and in detail, you will have to work on many different kinds of examples for a long time, to build up a detailed anatomy of mind. What I am doing here is to provide you with a map.

When I turn to the other clues I begin to go through all the stages that we have identified already. First I study the data in experience. I read the clues carefully. 2. J.A.S.O.N.— (8) and 4. HIJKLMNO (5). I feel in myself a feeling of resistance. They look more difficult.

They look like those tests of intelligence that psychologists give people. My imagination begins to work. "Name, JASON, Jason and the Golden Fleece, how many letters in fleece, six, no good." The images provide the immediate data on which the insights arise. Thus, "Jason went on a trip, what was the name of his ship, the Nautilus, no, that wasn't it. Argonauts, that was the name of the film, the one with the skeletons. Argonaut, that has eight letters." This is an insight emerging from a flow of images. As such it is just a possibility: it could be right or it could be wrong. We shall have to wait and see. Immediately I go on to check it by trying to fit it in with rum. No, it does not fit. Anyway, that does not explain why all the letters are capitals and why there are dots. The right answer has to explain all the relevant data. I turn to the last clue. 4. HIJKLMNO (5) This is a section of the English alphabet running in sequence. I notice that I run through the letters over and over again in my imagination. I try to pronounce the letters as a word: higkelmeno. I ponder that image: waiting to see whether it will spark off anything in the way of an insight. No. I am aware of great tension and tightness as I cast around desperately for an idea. I am acutely aware of a desire to know not liking to be frustrated. I go back to rum, just to console myself. Then, back to J.A.S.O.N.— Why are the dots there? This question arises from my scrutiny of the data. I find my imagination running through the letters. A new question arises. Is it a sequence based on the numerical place of the letters in the alphabet so that a=1, b=2, etc.? I race ahead to work out conditions for that being the right answer. If so, then the answer has to be another letter: so which letter has eight letters in it? My imagination skims through the alphabet and ends up with W. How do you spell W? With the fingers of one hand I count off double on the table, six letters. Then the U sound has to be spelt either u or you or ewe: (imagination: ewe, fleece?) but neither spelling gives me eight letters. My inquiry returns to the dots. Why are they there? What do they mean? My imagination runs through the series again saying dot after each one: J dot, A dot, . . . Nothing. Then, another insight occurs. I remember from my reading, e.g. e dot, g dot. One image sparks off another and the result is an insight. "Aha!" At once that spills out into words: "The dot stands for an abbreviation. It means that there is a whole word and they are only giving the initial." Back to the data. J.A.S.O.N.—. Another insight: it must be a familiar series of things abbreviated and the last one has to be put in where the dash is, and it has eight letters. My imagination is spurred on and inspired by this insight and begins to run through some series: "One, two, three, . . ." An insight: there are no numbers beginning with j. J for John, maybe it is evangelists, no, there are only four; apostles — James, Andrew, Simon, O for . . .? N for . . .? No. Familiar series. I notice how my imagination is pliable and ready to respond to the hints from inquiry. I think: learning by rote, children's mnemonics. What series do children learn? Memory supplies: thirty days has September . . . I notice that January begins with J. January, February, March . . . No. The days of the week. I run through them. No. Atomic elements? O for oxygen, N for nitrogen, nothing! My imagination represents again for me: Thirty days has September, April, June and November. I get an insight. S for September, A for April, J for June, N for November. They are all letters in the clue. I return to the clue again. I try to apply the insight to check whether it fits all the data. June, April, September, O-something, "October"?, November. That is not right, still, September, . . . A new insight. "I've got it!" September, October, November, December. It must be months of the year. J must be June, no it can't be, it has to be July. That's it: July, August, September, October, November, December! Now I feel the release of tension as I achieve a new insight. And the joy, the delight of understanding. Notice here also how the insight tumbles out into expression. Notice, too, how the insight is not seeing more, but is something totally different. It is a grasp of the invisible pattern or order that is the cause of the visible bits being the way they are.

I find that as soon as the insight has been formulated I rush to check whether it fits. As soon as I have expressed its content I appreciate that it is merely possible. I ask, Is it really the correct answer? I go ahead to work out the conditions that would have to be fulfilled if it were to be the correct answer. If it has eight letters, and if it fits in with RUM. Next I rush ahead to see whether these conditions are in fact fulfilled. I write in the letters of December: it has the correct number of letters and its M matches the M of RUM. At this point further act of understanding occurs. Do you notice this in yourself?

9. *Judging.*
Our doing of the crossword puzzle tends always to run ahead of the attempt to make a helpfully neat list of all the distinct parts of our knowing. We have distinguished the working out of the conditions which would have to be fulfilled in order for that answer to be not

only possible but also actually and really the correct one, and the working out whether these conditions are actually fulfilled. Now we have to draw attention to a final act of understanding. As soon as I have discovered that in fact the conditions are fulfilled, I reach a new kind of understanding called judging, in which I conclude "Yes!, That's it." In this act of judging I go beyond what I see, hear, touch, taste or smell, beyond what I feel or perceive, beyond what appears to be, seems to be, might be or could be, beyond what is possible, to know what actually, really and truly *is*.

As before, the tiny explosion of understanding in judging is so swift that it is all too easy to miss it, and so to misunderstand it. As before, we get some assistance by examining the act that comes after it.

10. *Expressing what is judged in a judgement.*

As an insight into a possibility is followed by a further act in which the content of that act is expressed, so an act of judging that something is the case is also followed by a further act in which the content of that act is expressed in a proposition or statement, or even in an exclamation. It is necessary to go through several examples before you will notice the various aspects of these acts.

This act of judging and its expression in judgement win for human knowing a remarkable prize, an end-product that is objective. The first level of insight yields a mental synthesis that is possible: it is a mental construct which might be the principle or ordering pattern that underlies the data experienced. The second level of insight, ending in judging and the formulation of judgement asks whether the synthesis formed in the mind corresponds to the ordering pattern that underlies and organises the experienced data: and having raised that question it works out what conditions would have to be fulfilled if that mental synthesis were to correspond to the actual ordering pattern in the data, and then it works out that these conditions are in fact fulfilled, and that therefore the synthesis constructed in and by the human mind does correspond to the actual ordering pattern of the experienced data.

What we have presented here is no more than a baby step in performance analysis: its aim is to show you that the way we know as human persons is open to analysis, an analysis that takes as its data, our own conscious experience of our acts of knowing. It is obviously not a full analysis: but it indicates the way in which a more adequate analysis may be carried out if you so wish.

We realise now that human knowing is not like taking a look: it is a structured process with several different parts which fit together in a particular order to build up a single piece of knowing. Only when they are fitted together properly do we know what *is*. Each earlier part calls forth the one after it and builds on the parts that came before it. And the extraordinary thing is that the end-product is a knowledge of what really, truly and actually *is*: when we know, we know, not just a mental synthesis constructed by and in our minds, but in and through such a mental construction we know a particle or facet of *being*, of what really, truly and actually *is*. Human knowing is a being-reaching device. This is such an amazing discovery that we shall pause a while to explore it and tease out a few of its literally earth-shattering implications.

A DESIRE TO KNOW AND LOVE BEING

We have had to spend time climbing the dry cliff of examining the way we know because such a violent storm rages about the nature of human knowing in our day and has such serious consequences for the way we live and shape our society. The great slogan of the cultural elites which control our education systems, especially at third level, is that human knowing is only relative or subjective: by this they mean that all we are able to know is our own opinion, that we are just unable to go beyond what *we* happen to think to reach what really, truly and actually *is*. The ideological elites say that human knowing is closed: we cannot get outside our minds by knowing and thereby reach reality, objective truth, being.

I have never been able to swallow this. After all, the very fact that modern technology works, that fridges, lifts, radios, televisions, hearing aids, asthma inhalers, and so on, actually work, proves to me that human knowing not only can but massively *has* worked. If the knowledge of botany and biochemistry was only subjective relative opinion, then the spray to kill the fungus would not work. But over and over again it does work. Therefore, that knowledge at least is more than a subjective relative opinion.

We can, however, ask how human knowing is more than a subjective, relative opinion, how, that is, we go beyond what we think to what is; and that is what we have done in the preceding part. We found that human knowing is indeed subjective, insofar as it happens only in someone's mind, and not anywhere else. But we found also that as well as the first step in which the mind constructs possible mental syntheses in the effort to understand the data experienced, there is also the second step in which the mind goes about verifying whether this or that possible mental synthesis corresponds to the actual structure ordering the data.

We want to go on now to ask about the driving force behind this amazing human capacity: what is it in us that pushes ahead the effort to know?

At first we have to say that it seems to be a desire of some kind. A desire for what? Well, not for food or drink, not for comfort or pleasure, not for power or fame, not for success or riches. It is a desire to know.

When we study animals we discover that their different kinds of activities seek special kinds of objectives or goals. That type of movement is for getting food; this noise is part of the mating behaviour; and so on. We discover what drives them by watching their actions and trying to understand the goals they are seeking. We study ourselves in a similar way, with the important difference that whereas with animals we can only study their outsides, that is to say, their behaviour as data that we experience through our senses, when we study ourselves we have not only that external data, but also we have the more immediate data of consciousness: we can study human action and passion from within by studying our own conscious acts.

When we study ourselves we find that we have many drives and desires similar to those we understand to be in the higher animals. But that is not all we find. We also find that we have this additional drive that is not to be found in the animals, and that we do this series of different kinds of actions that the animals do not do. What is the significance of this finding?

It means that we are not animals. We are a different kind of being. And since there is more in us than there is in them, we have to say that we are a higher kind of being.

It is a sign of the decadence into which public opinion and the academic elites have fallen today that it is necessary to labour this point. But it is necessary. Time and time again, I have discovered that people, and especially those suffering from third level education, find it difficult if not impossible to accept, let alone understand, that we are not animals.

What is it, then, that is in us but not in the animals? It is the desire to know and love being. We have examined briefly our knowing in this section and in the following sections we shall examine human love and action. Already, however, we have found that

■ there is a drive in us that underlies and pushes ahead the different kinds of acts that we spontaneously do when knowing, and that pushes the process of knowing ahead from one kind of act to the next;

■ this drive is experienced, once it is awakened, as a desire, a conscious desire; we want and we are aware of wanting;

■ this desire is a desire to know; what we want is to know; what we do is know; knowing is the end towards which the different kinds of act drive;

■ this desire is a desire to know being; we are not satisfied, and we do not rest, until we have gone beyond what seems to be, what might be, what is our opinion, what suits us to think, what could possibly be the case, to reach what really, truly and actually *is*; this desire heads spontaneously towards what *is* and is satisfied only by that; the desire to know drives us to go beyond what is possible to discover what in fact *is*, to know being.

Not only is human knowing a construction industry, not only may we say that the human mind is a being-reaching device, we have to go further and recognise that each of us is a desire to know being! The implications of this seemingly innocuous statement are explosive, but for the moment we shall just note it in passing as one of our discoveries on our journey: later on we shall see how huge are its consequences.

A SELF-ASSEMBLING DESIRE THAT ASSEMBLES ITS CONSTRUCT

Once this desire is awakened it assembles itself part by part; each part calls forth the next and operates spontaneously in relation to the last in a characteristic manner. The desire drives the process ahead from each lower level of activity to the level immediately above it, and fits all the parts together to make a full piece of knowing.

In doing so, however, it also assembles part by part, its proper construct, a new piece of human knowledge, the knowledge of a particle or aspect of being; in the example we took, the answers to some crossword puzzle clues. As the knowing assembles itself to build up a complete act of knowing, so its component acts produce their proper partial products which build up into a full construct, a new piece of human knowledge. And the staggering thing is that when we have gone through all these acts, the resulting piece of knowledge is objective: we have gone beyond what we think to know to what really, truly and actually is.

A UNILATERAL DECLARATION OF INDEPENDENCE

The answers Rum and December are correct. They are correct, not just because we say so, but because they are correct. Incredible as it may seem to the relativists and subjectivists of the cultural elites, our human knowing produces an objective result! How can this be?

First of all, do you share the difficulty of the relativists? Or at least, can you see where they find the difficulty? They say that human knowing is subjective. They are half right. It is true that our knowing is subjective insofar as it is done by a person, it is present in a person's mind and nowhere else: remember the discussion of the meaning in a book or a word. Human knowledge is a synthesis constructed in and by the human mind: and it is true that truth, human knowledge, exists nowhere else than in the judgements which are in people's minds. Thus far we are in agreement: human knowledge is subjective.

But they are wrong insofar as they go on to deny that human knowing is also objective. In fact it is both: it is subjective in that it is made in a mind and exists only in the judgements which are to be found nowhere else but in a mind; but it is also objective, insofar as when we reach a judgement, we are declaring precisely this, that the subjective construct made in and by the mind corresponds to the pattern ordering the experienced data. The act of judgement not only concludes that the conditions which would have to be fulfilled if the mental synthesis were to correspond to the pattern ordering the data, are in fact fulfilled, but also recognises and posits the piece of knowledge thereby reached as true, independent of the fact that it is I who have discovered it to be so.

Consider again the answer to the clues. What is it that makes them the right answers? Is it the fact that you or I worked them out? Surely not. What makes them the right answers is that they, and they alone, account for all the data. They fit. They meet the conditions. Is that not so? Well, then, that is what I mean when I say that human knowing is objective. What happens in judging is that we conclude that because the conditions are in fact fulfilled, therefore the piece of knowledge is valid, quite apart from the fact that you or I happen to have understood it to be so. Human knowing is subjective and objective. If somebody says to you, "Ah well, that is just your opinion: it is all relative," go back to the example: why is December the right answer? Is it just an opinion? Is it relative? It is the right answer because it accounts for the data. It is the right answer even if I never discovered it. What is relative is the fact that I happen to have discovered it. There is no necessity in that. I need not have found the crossword puzzle in the first place. I might not have had the right images to help me work out the answer. These are all things that are not necessary. But 'relative', here, then, has to mean what need not happen but as a matter of fact could happen and sometimes has happened. In that clearly defined sense of the word relative it makes sense to say that there are aspects of relativity to human knowing. But that in no way contradicts the fact that when we judge, we are announcing our awareness that we have reached the conclusion that the mental synthesis constructed in and by our mind corresponds to the pattern ordering the data, and that this is the case even if we had never understood it. When we say "Yes, I've got it!" we mean that December fits the clues, and the spaces, and fits in with the other answer, Rum; and we mean that it would be the right answer even if we had never set eyes on the wretched puzzle.

Human knowing, thus, is not only subjective but also objective. This objectivity has several parts. On the level of experience there is the sheer givenness of the data: we see what is there to be seen.

Next, when we have constructed a possibility and are striving to discover whether it fits the data, we experience human intelligence spontaneously acting in accordance with inbuilt norms of reasoning. For example, we reasoned in the crossword puzzle that if the first letter in Three Down was e, then eight could not be the right answer and seven had to be it. Here is a further element of objectivity: spontaneously, human intelligence is driven to act according to its own inherent norms of reasonableness. When we reason, 'if this, then that', 'if this is impossible, then that is necessary', we attain the second part of objectivity, where the truth of the norms is immediately self-evident to human intelligence.

Finally, and most astonishingly, we reach a judgement. When we do so, we bring to a close the work of discovering whether the conditions which would have to be fulfilled if the mental synthesis constructed in and by the mind were to correspond to the pattern ordering the data, are in fact fulfilled. We do this by bringing together the data given in experience with their element of objectivity, and the reasoning that works out conditions and tests their fulfilment with its element of objectivity, and by reaching the conclusion that the mental synthesis does correspond to the pattern ordering the data. In so doing, the human mind makes a unilateral declaration of independence: it declares I have found that this is the right answer, quite apart from the fact that I have found it to be so. It understands that the answer is true independent of my having found it to be so. The independence is onesided: for the mind is not independent of the truth in the way that the truth is independent of the mind. Unless the crossword puzzle had been invented and unless I had come across it, I could never have understood it. This is the most remarkable part of our knowing, this nonchalant declaration by the human mind that its mental construct is a circumscribed matter-of-fact absolute. And the whole fabric of human knowledge is made up of stitches each of which is one of these tiny matter-of-fact absolutes, a judgement.

This word absolute gives a lot of trouble so it is important to be clear about the way in which it is being used here. Some absolutes are necessary, others are matter-of-fact: we mean the second type, the matter-of-fact absolutes. A necessary absolute is something which is, and cannot not be: such are some of the laws in logic and mathematics, for instance, $2+2=4$. A matter-of-fact absolute is something which need not be, but which as a matter of fact, happens to be. Like our crossword puzzle: it need never have been invented, but it was. On the one hand, we recognise that it need not have existed: on the other, we also recognise that since it does exist, it is absolutely true to say that it exists; but we are intelligent, so we distinguish between different meanings of the word absolute and we qualify the type of absolute by calling it matter-of-fact. Now human knowledge is made up of judgements each of which is a matter-of-fact absolute, because each of us can know that we are matter-of-fact beings, we do exist, but we can find no reason why it is necessary that we exist: all we can say is that because certain conditions happen to have been fulfilled, we happen to exist. Again, our knowing any particular thing is not necessary: we can find no necessary reason why we should have to encounter any particular being at any time: as a matter of fact we do run into particular things at particular times and get to know some of them. And when we do so, in the act of judging in which we conclude that the relationships we have constructed in our mind do correspond with the order in what we have met, we are aware that what we have understood is true quite independently of our having discovered it to be so: it is an absolute, but a matter-of-fact absolute: in other words, we conclude, if these conditions had not been fulfilled, then it would not have been true; but as a matter of fact they were fulfilled, so as a matter of fact it happens to be true.

As the apple-tree has finished its work when it has produced a fully ripe apple that can be plucked and eaten, so the human mind has finished its work when it has produced a fully objective result that is recognised as true independent of our having found it to be so. In reaching that kind of result the mind is satisfied; the desire to know is satisfied. In knowing such an object we are also knowing a particle or aspect of being. This brings us to the question, What does it mean for us to know being? We are coming through the densest part of the journey to the Centre of the person at this stage: the analysis of knowing was the hardest part; the rest should be somewhat easier, as we tease out the unthinkable implications of what we have found.

TO KNOW SOMETHING IS TO BECOME ONE WITH IT

We have noticed already how imagination is an enthusiastic but misleading helper. Unless we take care it can mislead us into picture-thinking. When we wonder what knowing is like we are inclined to imagine that it must be like taking a look. Again, when we wonder what judging and verifying are like, our imagination throws up a mischievous image of the mind opening a little door in the side of my head and looking out to check whether the picture inside matches the data outside. In both of these cases, our imagination throws up the image of knowing as a meeting or encounter between the knower and what is known: knowing, we are tempted to conclude, is nothing more than a confrontation. But all along we have found that those who use this ominous phrase 'nothing more than' usually leave out something important: and that is the case here also. On the bodily level I confront the things that touch and activate my senses. But in the process of knowing I move up to another, deeper level of contact, something beyond confrontation.

In the list of parts of our knowing, two parts stand out as central:

they are the ends towards which the other acts drive and aim. They are understanding and judging. As far as the desire to know is concerned, experiencing, inquiring, questioning and playing with images are all done with a view to precipitating the outburst of insight, the little explosion of understanding. Again, when the content of that insight has been expressed, the desire to know strives to verify it, and all the subsequent work of ascertaining conditions and checking whether or not they are fulfilled is for the purpose of reaching the act of judging. These are the central acts, understanding and judging: the other acts prepare for them or express them.

To follow the next step in the journey you have to pay close attention to the act of understanding. We discover that while the preparatory activities do have a confrontational structure, the same is not the case for the act of understanding. Up to the instant at which we achieve insight we are examining images and sense-data. But, precisely at the moment of understanding, that ceases to be the case. In fact, the act of insight leaves behind the very material elements that we had been confronting. In the crossword puzzle we gave the example of a flow of images in which I was running through the numbers from one to ten. When the flash of understanding came, it left the images far behind and leapt to something else. The same happened in the case of the flow of images in the rhyme for remembering how many days there are in the various months. Before the insight arrives we are studying the words on the page and the images in our imagination. When insight strikes it leaves the images behind, although it does return to them soon afterwards. In the act of understanding itself, however, something other than confrontation is taking place. What is it?

We discovered that what we do in the act of understanding is construct a mental synthesis, a possible arrangement, relationship or order. Recall, again, the utter difference between looking at the clues and grasping the answer. They are totally different kinds of act. No amount of looking turns itself into an act of understanding. Before I have understood, the relationship I am seeking is just not in my mind: afterwards, it is. The intelligiblity that was in the crossword puzzle clues, or to be more accurate, in the mind of the person who invented it, in the act of understanding comes to be in my mind. Before I have understood, it is not in my mind, so I study data and images. The images spark it off in my mind. But once it is in my mind, I no longer need the images or the data in order to understand it, because it is in my mind as an act of understanding!

To know something, then, is to become one with it. The same form that was in the clue is now formed by my mind in itself. This is not confrontation: my mind is not looking at anything. My mind is activated by the identical form that was in the mind of the crafty crossword puzzle maker. It is like the way a string on a guitar hums when the corresponding note is played on a piano nearby. What an extraordinary thing the human mind is! It is not satisfied with confronting and scrutinising the outsides of things. In an amazing manner the human mind takes things inside itself by reproducing their inner form within itself. It has the capacity to form in itself the forms of the things around it. It becomes the inner forms of these things in a non-material manner.

We understand the answers to the crossword puzzle clues without becoming paper and ink, without becoming a crossword puzzle, without becoming the person who thought it up. In the act of under-standing there is not confrontation but a becoming one with the thing understood. It is a sympathetic in-formation, if we may speak in this way. In understanding, my mind becomes the thing under-stood in a non-material manner by forming in itself the form of that thing. In understanding, the mind reaches an intentional identity with the thing understood in a non-material manner.

THE MEANING OF THE WORD 'SPIRITUAL'

Thus, at last, we have arrived at the delicate and fleeting experience that enables us to give a precise meaning to that most important word 'spiritual'. Central to the recovery of our true identity, and to the nature and destiny of the whole journey on which we are engaged, is the insight that <u>we are spiritual as well as bodily beings.</u>

But in our day, the meaning of the word 'spiritual' has been lost under immense avalanches of ideological and fundamentalist abuse. The whole of the journey up to this point has had this goal in mind, to enable us to pinpoint exactly the human experience on which the word 'spiritual' rests. And this is it. At the centre of the process of knowing which distinguishes us from the animals is the tiny outburst of insight, the explosion of understanding. It is on this experience that the meaning of the word 'spiritual' hinges: it is from an under-standing of this experience, and its implications for the rest of our being, that the word 'spiritual' radiates.

Just before the occurrence of insight, the mind strains and struggles to reach the pattern hidden in the data and in the flow of images. These images are the partially de-materialised representations of the data given in experience. In the explosion of understanding, however, the mind tosses aside even these light crutches because it needs them no longer. In the act of understanding the mind forms in itself the form that was in the images and in the data. In this act of in-formation, the mind becomes one with the thing it was trying to understand, but in a non-material way. The special word for this non-material manner of intentional identity between the knower and the known is 'spiritual'. The spiritual is the non-material. And where do we experience ourselves performing a non-material activity? Whenever we understand anything. Why do we call it non-material? Because, as we can check in our own experience, since these acts are conscious, in the instant of understanding, the mind goes beyond even the image, the last vestige of materiality, and forms in itself the form of the thing it seeks to understand.

When we examined imagination we asked about its object: it seemed to be twofold, the image itself and the thing to which the image referred. When we ask what the object of human knowing is, we meet a similar apparent difficulty. Our imagination insists on introducing the picture of knowing as something like a look: are there, we wonder, two objects, an external and an internal? How could we know an external object by looking at an internal one? To correct this intrusion of imagination we have to recall that the mind makes something in and through which it knows the external object; or, to be more precise, the mind becomes the form of the thing, it forms that form immaterially within itself.

THE HUMAN SPIRIT

We have been referring to the mind as an 'it'. We should now correct that imprecision. The mind is not an 'it' that is in me like my dinner in my stomach: it is me. It is I who understand. And what an extra-ordinary act understanding is! I in-form in my mind in a spiritual, that is to say, non-material manner, the form of the thing I want to know. What is the source of this astonishing act? Where does it come from? What exactly is the human mind that it is able to turn itself, first into one thing, then into another, and then into yet another? Has it no form of its own, that it must always be taking on the forms of other things?

We have found that as soon as it is awakened, we experience it as a voracious desire to know, a ravenous appetite for understanding. Now we make a further discovery: we are not able to observe directly what this drive is like before it is awakened. When we are acting, doing some knowing, then we can observe it. But apart from this, before that, it is not present to us consciously.

Does this mean, then, that we can know no more about it? No! Because, as we have found, knowing is not just taking a visual look: it may start from a look, but then it goes ahead to perform further actions which form additional elements that go beyond what we see, to construct a piece of knowledge. And the same happens in the case of our consciousness of an act of understanding. Being aware of doing an act of understanding is one thing: we are able to make that awareness the data with which we begin to perform further acts of knowing. We start from that awareness and then go ahead to perform further actions which form additional elements that go beyond what we are aware of, to construct a piece of knowing. In other words, we take what is given in our awareness when the desire to know is active as data. Then we proceed to build up new knowledge in which we add to that data insights into what the desire to know is like before it acts.

When it is awakened by data or images, we experience the mind as a desire to know. When we understand something, we discover that the mind performs a spiritual act in which it becomes one with the form of the thing known in a non-material way. Now we ask: what form does the mind have before being in-formed when knowing something? The answer is somewhat odd; it seems to have no form of its own. Slowly we understand what it is. The human mind is a pure capacity to understand, a sheer ability to know, a bare power or potentiality to become one with any form presented to it by the data of sense or consciousness. It is not that it does not have a form of its own, but that its form is non-material: it has, or more accurately is, a spiritual form. It is a mere capability able to be in-formed by any form whose sensible aspects impinge on my senses. Even when it is not acting, when it is not in-forming in an act of knowing, it is still present and active, because as soon as suitable materials touch the senses and intrigue the imagination, it awakens as desire to know.

We have been referring, again, to an 'it': what is this 'it'? It is part of me. What part? Not a material part: so, then, a non-material part, a spiritual part. What does that mean? What kind of source is in me that produces spiritual acts like understanding? From what within me does this spiritual act of understanding spring?

When we examined the difference between the activities of a plant and those of a mere heap of sand, we observed that the plant has a sequence of different structures at different stages in its lifespan: we understood that what distinguishes a plant from a random and unrelated collection of pieces is the existence within it of an inner plan or form according to which it unfolds and acts: this inner plan or form governs the sequence of increasingly developed structures that occur during its growth. Unlike the house that is built according to an external plan by an external builder, the plant is a self-operating, self-assembling being. We then discovered that we had to say more. The plant is a self-operator, a self-assembler, a self-developer: and that is precisely what is meant by saying that it is alive, that it is a living being.

We have to follow a similar line of discovery here. In the human being we readily observe the sequence of different structures that characterise the various stages of human bodily life from conception to maturity. Here, too, we discover an inner plan or form which governs or directs the unfolding of the beautiful sequence of stages during development. The human being, we understand, is a self-operating, self-moving, self-assembling, self-developing unity. And here, too, we discover that we have to say more: the human being is a self-operator, a self-mover, a self-assembler, a self-developer. Each of us has within himself or herself the principle of his or her own operation and growth, his or her own life. Each of us is a living human being.

As soon as we hear this word 'within', as soon as we say that the human being has its own principle of activity and living within itself, we start to pay attention, because we have found that human beings are characterised by a special kind of 'within-ness' that we have called consciousness. Human beings are able to experience their 'within-ness' immediately in their consciousness. This means that a further avenue of exploration is open to us in the attempt to study the principle of human living and activity. We do not have to stop at the outside, as we had to in the case of plants and animals, we can study this principle as it is given to us in our consciousness.

When we begin to do so, the first discovery we make is what we may call the experienced unity of consciousness: I am conscious that it is the same me who feels tired and hungry, and who inquires and understands: there are not given in my consciousness, several me's, one of whom does the bodily actions and feelings, and another who takes care of knowing and loving. No. It is the same, single consciousness that is aware of performing my bodily as well as my spiritual activities. From this we understand that both the bodily activities and the spiritual activities spring from the same principle in me: and that corresponds exactly to the data of consciousness: I am well aware that it is the same me who sees and who understands.

The next discovery we make is that human knowing also has an inner plan or form which governs and directs the unfolding of the several different kinds of act that go to make up a piece of knowing. Human knowing, we discover, is a self-operating, self-moving, self-assembling, self-developing process. And here, too, we find that we are driven to say more: we have to say that human knowing springs from a self-operator, a self-mover, a self-assembler, a self-developer; and that spring or source of knowing, the principle of the process of knowing, is the knower, the person himself or herself. It is I who know.

But, and here is the startling discovery, since the act of understanding is spiritual, it follows that the source, the spring, the principle, from which this act originates and flows, the desire to know, and the capacity behind it, this, too, is spiritual. But it is not sufficient merely to say that it is spiritual, that I am spiritual: we have to go one step further.

As the life of the plant or animal consists in the fact that it is not only self-operating, but also *a self-operator,* so the source of human knowing is not only spiritual, but is *a human spirit*: I am *a human spirit*; you are *a human spirit.*

The human person, then, is not only a body but also a spirit. And since, as we have already discovered, it is the same I who eats and walks as inquires and understands, we have to be on our guard against the clumsy help offered by our imagination which immediately throws up pictures of a little man inside a big man's body, as if I were inside my body in the same way that I am inside my shirt. Against these misleading pictures presented by our imagination we have to insist on what we have discovered in our own conscious experience, that it is the same I who breathes, digests, circulates blood, grows, sees, hears, tastes, touches, smells, moves about, gets hungry and eats, thirsty and drinks, tired and sleeps, dreams, feels pain and pleasure, irritation and affection and undergoes or performs all the passions and actions linked to the human body, and who plays freely with images, inquires, questions, understands, conceptualises and defines, creates language and speaks and reads and writes, reasons and judges, loves and evaluates, chooses freely and acts responsibly, works and plays, creates artistically and potters about in the garden, makes friendships and undertakes lifelong commitments that involve suffering and self-sacrifice, and asks deep questions about the meaning of it all: it is the same I. I am at once body and spirit: I am aware of this identity immediately from my experience. The truth of this identity can be brought home to anyone who denies it by standing on their toe when they are not looking: when they inquire "Who stood on my toe?" you can point out to them that in this question they have expressed their experience that it is the same I who feels the toe and the assault thereupon, and who raises the question of the name of their assailant: the pain experienced in the toe is on the level of sensitive consciousness: the inquiry is on the level of inquiring consciousness: it is the same I who has both levels of consciousness. From this it follows that the human spirit is the principle of the life and activities of the human body.

We asked earlier what the desire to know does before it is awakened. We observed that before it has been awakened we do not experience it at all. So where is it? Where has it gone? Again, we noticed that in the act of understanding I in-form in my mind the form of whatever is presented to my senses and imagination by my body: my mind seemed to be able to take on the form of whatever it met. We asked: has it no form of its own? What form does it have when it is not taking on the form of anything else? It seems to vanish when it is not actually understanding something else.

The problem, here, is that we are finding it difficult to go beyond the image of knowing as like taking a look: when our eye is not looking, the eye itself is still there and we can see it. What is left 'still there' when the desire to know is not awakened? And where is it? Once we make the effort to go beyond that picture we realise that the form of our understanding, our desire to know, its 'own' form, as distinguished from the forms of the things it understands, is a pure capacity to understand: and we cannot make a satisfactory picture of it precisely because it is spiritual, non-material.

But when we push this line of inquiry a little further we make a further discovery. When a candle is not burning, where is the flame?

The answer seems to be that unless it is actually burning something, the flame ceases to exist. It seems as if the same might be true for the capacity to understand. If I am not actually understanding anything, then how does the pure capacity to understand survive from one awakening to the next? To answer this question we have to get away from picture-thinking once again and back to our own experience.

We know from our own experience that we are not understanding continuously: for example, we go to sleep. But our experience also tells us that when I wake up today, I am aware that I am the same I who went to sleep yesterday. The I worries during breakfast this morning how on earth I am going to find the money to pay the bills accumulated during that impetuous shopping spree done by the same I yesterday afternoon. The same I does the worrying as did the spending. The fact of identity is given immediately in consciousness.

The question, then, is not whether such an identity exists, but how it can exist. Where does my desire to know go when I am asleep? How does it continue to exist when it is not doing any understanding? Just as we had to go further than the discovery that the act of understanding and its source in me are spiritual, so too here we have to go further than the discovery that behind these acts is a capacity: just as we had to recognise the existence of the human spirit, so too we have to recognise that this capacity to understand is something that exists, that the human spirit which has this capacity is something that exists. We found that an adjective like spiritual is not adequate to describe its substantiality; we needed a noun, the human spirit. Now we have to stress that this is not just a verbal matter. The human spirit with its capacity to understand is a substantial reality that exists in its own right: it is the subsistent form of the human being as a whole.

We may observe in passing that our imagination is left somewhat breathless by this discovery because it has been left behind: we do not experience what the human spirit with its capacity to understand is like when it is not in action: in the discovery of the spirit and its capacity to understand we are going beyond experience. But that is precisely what happens when we do a piece of knowing: we go beyond experience to reach something unlike what is given in experience. And this happens also in the case of knowing the human spirit.

This analysis has important practical implications for the way we regard and treat people who are in a coma. When a person is asleep or in a coma, or has suffered irreversible brain-damage such that there is no natural possibility of the brain being repaired and so no possibility of the imagination operating and presenting images to awaken the desire to know, nonetheless, as long as the person is alive, he or she is a human being, a living unity of body and spirit, in which the human spirit is operating as the principle of the bodily living and activities like blood-circulation, breathing, digestion and all the other involuntary activities: the capacity to understand is still present but is unable to act naturally in the absence of images. Such a person is just as much a human being as you or I. It is incorrect to say that such a person is a vegetable: he or she is a full human person who, due to damage to the body, is unable to engage in conscious activity in the natural manner.

THE VIEW FROM THE CLIFF-TOP

We have arrived at long last at the cliff-top. Let us pause for a moment to drink in the view. We have undertaken a journey into the human person in order to challenge the dominant view of what we are. The main characteristic of that dominant view is its denial of the openness and infinity of the human person.

We drew on the symbol of depth to hint at the presence within each of us an inner space that is in some way fathomless, unlimited. As children we were told that if we dropped a stone over a cliff and counted the number of seconds before we heard it hit the bottom, we could calculate the length of the drop. Our journey has been a series of pebbles tossed into the depths of the human person: we have been straining to hear the splash that marks the depth. We begin now to appreciate why we have heard no splash: we have radically under-estimated the depth of the person. Because the human body is small and calculable in size, we presumed that the same must be true for the human spirit. We accepted what the dominant opinion drums into us, that the human being is smaller on the inside than on the outside: now we begin to recognise the closedness of that opinion. The fact is that we are larger on the inside than on the outside. As the pebbles are still falling, so it takes a while for this new view of the human being to sink in: we have to mull over it, to explore its meaning slowly and to drink in its implications; to grow accustomed to considering the human person as in some sense infinite takes time.

We have hinted all along that the human person in some way is infinite. We drew attention to the common experience that our desire to know repeatedly overtakes each new stage of achievement: as soon

94

as we finish one piece of knowing, our mind races ahead to become interested in something else. We suggested that the unlimitedness of our questioning might in some way resemble the three dots that indicate an infinite series (2, 4, 6, 8, 10, . . .). We spoke of person-depth. Now we are in a position to understand more precisely what is meant by recognising the infinity of the human person.

Clearly, the infinity is not the infinity of actual accomplishment: none of us understands everything. Nor, is it the infinity of actual desire: I have never been aware of actually desiring to know every-thing: there are myriads of things that I do not even know about so I do not actually desire to know them. The infinity of the human mind does not lie in its achievement nor in its desire. But what else is there? Here we can draw upon the examination of the difference between the desire to know and the capacity to know. It is in the pure capacity to know that we can identify precisely the special sense in which we have to recognise the infinity of the human mind: it is infinite not in achievement nor in desire but in capacity. There is nothing in this pure capacity to prevent it from understanding one thing after another *ad infinitum*: what limits its performance is the limitedness of the body; we get tired and cannot work any longer or we get hurt and our body fails to function properly. As for the pure capacity itself, the forms that it in-forms in itself are present immaterially so there is no sense in which it can be said to be filled to the brim or reach saturation point. And while emotional wounds or selfish bad habits may block or misdirect the unfolding of the desire to know, experi-ence confirms that the thirst for understanding grows rather than diminishes with progressive accomplishment: the more we discover, the more we want to learn and explore. That is the experience in right order: the experience of stunted learning and of resistance to knowing is a deformation.

How wide, then, is the view from the cliff-top? The human spirit in each of us is, in part, a capacity to know unlimitedly, to know everything that exists, to know all being. It is a common experience that when we walk along a cliff-top for the first time, especially one as high as this, that we experience a dizziness, a vertigo. When we put into words the conclusion about the infinite thirst and thrust of the human mind we are likely to suffer from a similar vertigo. Surely, we think, this cannot be true: how can we be a capacity that is able to understand all being? Surely that is too much? We feel something like agoraphobia, the fear of open spaces. That is because for too long we have been locked up in the closed view of the person by the dominant opinions about knowing. We feel rather overwhelmed by the sheer immensity of the horizon that stretches out before us, much as a prisoner serving a life sentence in a solitary confinement in a small cell would feel if he were set free and placed on a high cliff-top. How are we to express the newfound extent of the mind? The word that sums it up best for me is open: the human mind is open; open in the sense that it is able to go beyond the opinions that suit my interest to reach what really, truly and actually is, to reach being; and open in the deeper sense that it is a capacity whose natural object is the whole of being, everything, everything that exists.

To help us find our feet against this vertigo, let us try to put it into words. Surely, we imagine, there might be things that lie outside the range of our puny power to know? Things, perhaps, so alien to us that we cannot even imagine what they are like? To answer that type of problem we have to recall what we found in the examination of the object of knowing. We discovered that the natural object of the desire to know is *that which exists*, being. Suppose, then, one of these things that we think might fall outside the range of our capacity to know; we can at least ask of it, What is it? What is it about it that places it outside the range of our power to know? Does it exist? If it does, then it is among the things that form the natural object of our power to know. If not, then we could not know it anyway, for the object of the capacity to know is what is, not what does not exist.

And, in fact, we have only to glance at the entertaining tales of science fiction to see how just this meeting between the human person and alien beings fascinates modern people: an indication, perhaps, of their dissatisfaction with the closed view of the human person, and of attempts to move outside that view.

This brings us to the end of the present section on human knowing. It is the most difficult part of the journey. The aim was to present a simple paradigmatic meditation to assist the recovery of the meaning of the human spirit and the human mind, at least a little. This path of inquiry is one of the lines of tradition central to Western civilization, and its recovery, I believe, is one of the most urgent tasks if there is to be a properly grounded resistance to the contemporary general collapses into ideology and fundamentalism and the underlying eclipse, deformation and contraction of spiritual experience. This path of inquiry was laid down by Plato and Aristotle, continued, recovered and developed by Augustine and Thomas, and in our day rediscovered and filled out by Bernard Lonergan and Eric Voegelin, on whose works my own exploration has been based.

We turn now to examine the other capacity of the human spirit, love.

LOVE

THE QUESTION ABOUT LOVE

And so at long last we arrive at love, surely the most human and personal of our activities: here, if anywhere, we should find the secret of personhood and the key to our opening and flowering. We are for love: where there is love, it is good to be: love is the heart of human-kind. We began the journey of self-exploration with a reflection on the significance of our names, their importance in how we see our-selves and feel about ourselves. But overwhelmingly, our identity is forged within our relationships: here is where we learn and are taught most effectively what we are and what we are worth. And what makes these relationships shape us in the right way is the presence in them as their spring and measure, of love. As I type this I seem to hear the chorus of cynics sigh over my shoulder, "Ah yes! Love! But of course it all depends on what you mean by love." And so it does. It is precisely the purpose of this section to examine what human love is, just as we examined human knowing in the previous section. And just as there was a storm raging about the meaning of knowing, so too we find that there is a storm, part of the same storm, in fact, over the meaning of love. In this storm our principal concern must be to avoid falling off the cliff which we took so long in ascending in the preced-ing pages. We must retain the discoveries that we made in that section and apply them here to the question about love.

And what is the question about love? When we speak of love, we speak also about the good, about goodness. What we love we call good and we say that we love it because it is good. The question about love, then, is this: is our love objective? Do we love something because it is really good, or do we merely call it good because we love it? As we found in the case of knowing, love is, of course, subjective. It is always some person or other who loves this or that good. Like instances of knowing, so too instances of love are found only in persons. The question, however, is: Is our love also, sometimes, objective? Is it the case that when we love something, not only do we like it because it gives us pleasure or is useful to us, but also because it is really, truly and actually good? Does the word good mean anything more than what gives somebody pleasure or convenience? Are the things we love really good, and is that why we are drawn to love them?

THREE KINDS OF GOOD THINGS

We found that when we have a question, our imagination often throws up an image for us that can help us part of the way towards understanding. We go beyond that image by asking further questions.

The first image that springs to mind is an apple. I love an apple! I like the taste: they are juicy and pleasant to eat. There is no doubt about it, apples are good. Is my liking subjective? Of course! It is I who like them. Is the liking only subjective? Hardly: for one thing, other people like them also; for another, it seems fairly indisputable that the structure of my body and the structure of the apple are such that the apple is an excellent nourishment. So, a first glance at the problem suggests that there is an objective correlation or aptitude between the human body and an apple, and a subjective conformation to that objective reality, I like the apple: and we are inclined to conclude that the objective correlation is the cause of the subjective relationship: I like the apple because it is good for me. So far so . . . good?

But we recognise other kinds of things as good even though we get no satisfaction from them directly. Thus, my enjoyment of the apple is brought about by a series of instrumental realities like roads and trucks, shops and cash registers, planes and airports, knives and tables, and so on. We recognise that these, too, are good, but in a different way: they are good because they bring about the things that we desire directly. And there are still other things that we recognise as good quite apart from whether or not they are useful to us or give us satisfaction: these are things which we recognise are good in themselves, for example, a human being. So, we have to distinguish three kinds of good things, desirable things, useful things and things that are good in themselves apart from any use or satisfaction that they may bring to us.

This carries us already a little beyond the image of the apple provided so helpfully by the imagination. How did I picture love in this image? The picture was of me placed in front of something that I wanted: love was the attraction that drew me to the thing. Love, the image suggested, is a desire for something I want but have not got. The limitation of this image is that rather than answer the question What is love? it pushes it back a stage: I desire this apple because I already like apples and want one now. The love had already set in before the wanting began.

The recognition of three kinds of good things carries us further still: among the three things, it seems in one way that desirable goods take precedence over useful goods, in the sense that I regard a supermarket as a good thing, not in itself, but because it is useful for bringing me things that I desire, like apples. We are able to sketch a crude order of priorities or ranking of kinds of good things: it seems to make sense to say that the apple is a higher kind of good than the road which brings it to me, because the road is an instrument or means by which the thing desired is brought to the one who desires it. Again, it seems obvious enough that I am a higher kind of good than the apple, because the apple is for me. So, a first attempt at constructing a scale of goods yields the following order of priority: things that are good in themselves are better than things that are good as objects of desire, which in turn are better than things which are instrumental in bringing objects of desire to people.

The example thrown up by imagination has a further difficulty in that it might suggest that whatever gives us pleasure is good, and thus, that good means what gives pleasure. That this is not the case is easily shown: sugar and chocolate give pleasure but may lead to tooth decay and overweight; alcohol produces a pleasant effect but can lead to drunkenness, alcoholic addiction, car crashes and domestic chaos and violence; heroin, we are told, gives pleasure but leads to addiction and can ruin lives. Again, what pleases me when I am healthy may revolt me when I am ill; and what pleases me in the right amount would sicken me in excess; again, what pleases me at one time may cease to do so at another. We are forced to recognise that pleasure alone is an insufficient guide to what is really good. Not everything that gives pleasure is good; sometimes what gives pain may be good, like dental treatment or a diet or training. This clears the way somewhat and helps me to see the kind of example that would avoid these two limitations of the apple example, the fact that I am desiring something that I already like, and the ambiguity of pleasure as an indicator of goodness. This ambiguity is linked to the fact that the liking is self-centred: it is I who do the wanting and I want the apple for myself. What I need is an example that gets away from this self-centredness. In such an example the nature of love might be clearer.

The best example I can find is minding our children. When I am minding them I am often called upon to leave aside what I want to do, and to do instead what they want to do. What I want to do is to sit by the big fire and get dug into this Agatha Christie that I am reading (for the third time). What they want is the red pencil which has somehow found its way onto the top of the wardrobe, a piece of sticky tape, two pins and some green wool. They firmly take my beautiful detective story and close it and then it's off to the wardrobe in pursuit of the lost pencil . . . Here the centre of my concern is not what I want but what they want. I want what they want. I am doing, not what gives me pleasure or satisfaction, nor what is useful to me, but what they want. Why? Because there is something in me that makes me ready to do what is good for them, in this instance, to play. And that something is love.

How does this example fit into the distinction of the three kinds of goods? Our children are good, not because of the satisfaction they give me, nor because of the use they are to me, now or later, but overwhelmingly and primarily because of the beings they are. We call them good because they are good. When I watch them my heart goes out to them. I do not murmur, "His muscles are going to be useful." Or "Everyone is going to praise me for her manners." Doubtless, I do derive immense enjoyment from them: and who knows, they might even prove useful to me in some way: but that is not why I regard them as good. Anyone who regarded his children as good for those reasons would be abnormal, deformed in a serious way. No. A child is good in himself or herself, for his or her own sake, quite apart from what their parents or anyone else thinks or feels about them. What fills my heart when I behold our children is a reverent awareness of their preciousness in themselves. The recognition of their goodness is the ground of the love I have for them. It is this love that leads me to postpone my enjoyment of the revelation of the significance of the crushed china teacup (for the third time) and go on the quest for the lost pencil.

This example enables us to distinguish two phases or moments in love, a first phase in which I love the children in themselves because of what they are, and a second phase in which that love leads me to undertake actions that seek what is good for them. The first we shall call being in love, and the second, loving action. As we did for knowing, we are going to try to examine an actual piece of loving in order to discover what love is. This is to enable you to do likewise and to examine in your own experience whether what I say corresponds to what you find in yourself.

LOVE'S BEGINNING

Of the two phases of love, the second is the easier to find in our experience: most of what we do each day is action related to things we love. In order to understand these actions properly we have to relate them back to the first phase of love, to what we are calling being in love. This first phase is not underlined as much in modern times and its neglect has contributed to a misunderstanding of the second phase, and more generally to the atmosphere of unease and anxious alienation that pollutes the climate of opinion so pervasively today.

In the example of the apple, it was impossible to get at the meaning of love because I could not recall the first occasion on which I met and began to like them. I have, however, a most vivid memory of the first time I met our first child, Ingrid, face to face. I remember well going into the Coombe Lying-In Hospital and taking her up into my arms for the first time. It is one of the sharpest and deepest memories that I have. Over me swept an awe, a depth-quake of acceptance, an overwhelming awareness of the preciousness of this tiny living being. Beautiful! Fragile! Perfect in extraordinary detail! But above all, precious! Good, not because she would give me pleasure or be useful to me, but good in herself, good because of what she was, who she was. No sooner had I set eyes on her and taken her up into my arms than my heart responded to her existence with a calm happy outburst of acceptance. This vast joyful yes to her being fell from my heart as spontaneously as a stone falls downwards. This newborn baby girl drew from me an affectionate 'yes to you': this tranquil, natural upsurge of affectionate consent to her being is the spring from which flows the stream of actions which seek the good things she needs.

Here is love's beginning. It is a conscious act so we are aware when it occurs and we can remember it and study it later. How are we to link this beginning of love to the analysis of the human person and of knowing in the previous section? The first point that comes to mind is that I notice in myself an uneasiness about using the word love to describe my wanting an apple when I have just used it for my response to our child. To call the desire for an apple love seems to trivialise the word: I am aware that the word love is used in a multitude of vague and overlapping ways, and is also much abused. The word needs to be salvaged from all this confusion and misuse. Such a salvage operation has to draw heavily upon what we discovered in the section on knowing. In particular, the many ways in which the word is used may be clarified by recalling that in the human being there is not only the body but also the spirit, and that as well as the several drives, passions and desires of the body there are also those of the human spirit. As a first hint we can say that there is in the human spirit, an appetite like the passion, desire, wanting and liking that are found in the human body.

When we ask what it is that this spiritual appetite desires, we have to answer that just as what the human mind desires is to know, so what the human heart desires is to love. And just as what the human mind desires to know is being, so, too, what the human heart desires to love is being. This explains why in the hierarchy of goods that we drew up earlier, the first place was given to things that are good in themselves. The first phase of love is that which loves things purely because they exist, as beings. Later, we may discover that they are also good because they bring us pleasure or are useful to us, but first we love them sheerly because they are.

Let us link this, now, with what we found about knowing. We found that human knowing begins from what it experiences and proceeds through inquiry, understanding, reflection and judgement to reach knowledge of a particle or aspect of being. Now we have to draw attention to a further conscious activity that occurs after judgement has taken place. As we noted already, this further activity is not massive or usually dramatic, so it is easy to miss. It is the act of acceptance with which I spontaneously greet and consent to the being that my knowledge has presented to me. After each act of knowing there occurs this quiet fleeting act of acceptance: after the mind has known a being, the heart accepts it. And this little act of the heart is love. What the mind knows to be, the heart loves. It is in order to focus attention on this little act that I selected the example of meeting my newborn daughter for the first time. In such an example, the act of love is the centre of attention and is easier to understand.

Love in its most essential form is this heart's yes to anything the mind has come to know as existing. It does not require that we know all about the thing we love: it is enough to know that it is, then the heart loves it. True, the more we know it the more we love it. But the essential characteristic of human love is the acceptance of what is known to exist. What, then, is the proper object of human love? It is being, any and every being: no sooner does the human mind know that something is, than the human heart is moved by that being to an act of passive consent. That is just the kind of being we are, we love beings, any and every kind of being. Once we begin to identify this responsive acceptance of a newly-known being it becomes clearer why this unobtrusive act is properly named love. Now that our attention has been drawn to it, we are able to recognise this fleeting act of appreciative acceptance of being. I remember my response to a single strand of a creeper climbing up the corner of a granite building, its leaves a brilliant Autumnal red; to a new song on the radio; to the magnificent voices of Laurence Olivier and Richard Burton; to bright dots of fungi on dead wood; to sea lettuce in a rockpool; to innumerable sunsets each with spectacular shades and colours; to the delicate and intricate cacti in the Botanical Gardens; to the design on the petals of London's Pride; to countless other things. . . No sooner do we come upon them than our hearts light up and exult in them.

Love's beginning is well described as falling in love. Falling is a good word to describe the ease and unforcedness of our heart's response to the beings we meet. As soon as we know that something *is,* we spontaneously and naturally fall for it, we are moved by it, stirred to the depths by it: we consent to it, we greet it. The word falling captures the effortlessness of this consent of the heart to the very being of something. It is unlike climbing that requires an effort: as the saying goes, it is as easy as falling off a wall.

As in the case of knowing, we find it difficult or impossible to recall the actual occasions on which we first met most things. But we can recall many other occasions on which we have met and fallen in love with ordinary and everyday things. The present-day uses and abuses of the word love obscure this first phase of love. But as we begin to heal the word from these wounds we begin to recognise this little act in which everything we meet moves us to receive it quietly and with admiration into our heart. We realise that this act is not dramatic or disruptive in most cases, but occurs so gently that, for the most part, we hardly notice it. It is an approval, a glorying in the marvellous being that we have found: how good this is!

And after the initial act of falling in love has taken place, it remains in our heart as a state of being in love with each being we have met. I am deliberately taking these phrases 'falling in love' and 'being in love' which are usually used to describe what happens between two persons, and applying them to what happens in every instance of a person meeting anything. This is because the act of love in its first phase is most clearly identifiable in love between people, while it is easily missed in the more ordinary meetings with mundane things like birds and napkins. Nonetheless, it is present also in these less dramatic cases and we need to understand it in order to understand the actions that flow from it.

This enables us also to recognise that everything is first and foremost a good in itself because it is a being, before it becomes an object of desire or an instrument because someone wants it. Everything, precisely insofar as it *is*, is good in itself.

Once we have identified this experience, the act of falling in love with things, we recognise a flood of such instances in our day-to-day living. For me, it is most vivid in the family. As the children reach each new stage, walking, teething, writing, reading, reasoning, hut-building, gang-forming, we report to one another with immense enjoyment the new dimernsions of these amazing beings which have just come to light, and we fall in love with each new step they take. And in their eyes we are able to relive the first falling in love with reality which is childhood: diligently they collect things, a worm, a moth ("a mop!"), a ladybird, and build homes in matchboxes so that they can 'mind' them. Piece by piece they construct a jigsaw of joy; each new thing known is loved. With each new thing known and loved a further stitch is added to this coat of many colours. And these stitches last: once we have fallen in love with things we remain in love with them. And this being in love with being is the basic attitude of the human person towards reality. We are in love with being. The different acts of falling in love with this and that do not remain separate but rather knit together into an all-embracing love for everything. And as we get to know more about things so we love them more.

Love in this first phase is not so much something we do to the thing we love, as something it does to us: we are moved by it, moved to receive and accept it affectionately. When we touch a sheet of glass with a finger we leave a fingerprint on it: when we know something, it moves us to love it; it leaves its loveprint on our heart. It imprints on our hearts a love for it, a likeness to it: it forms our heart in its own likeness. When we magnify a newspaper photograph it is made up of tiny dots of different shades: our attitude to the world is made up of loveprints stitched together. Our love is proportionate: I love some things more than others because they are better; a child is worth more than a mountain. So, in our lovescape, some things stand out as a foreground and others make up a background. Often we hear experts speak of us living in 'conditions'or 'environments': properly, inorganic realities exist under conditions and plants and animals live in environments: human persons live in a lovescape made by knowing and loving.

When we recognise the existence and nature of this little act of love, we are able to place it after the act of judging that concludes a piece of knowing. We identify many instances of it and appreciate how it fits in with our knowing: whatever we know, we then love. In the human spirit, thus, as well as the capacity to know that we have called mind, there is also a capacity to love, which we call heart. What the mind knows is being; so, too, what the heart loves is being. Each of us, therefore, is a desire to know and love being. But not a disembodied spirit, nor a spirit imprisoned in an alien body. We are human persons, each one a unity of body and spirit. Thus, we understand, not forms that float about on their own, but real things which have forms and our own images of these as represented in our imagination. And as we grasp the forms of things in images, so too when our heart loves things, it loves what the mind knows not coldly without emotion, but as presented in a context of feelings.

As in knowing we make ourselves one with what we know, so too in love we become one with what we love: not in a physical or material fusion, but in a spiritual union. Although love produces no inner object in the heart such as the concepts or judgements produced by the mind in knowing, it does leave in the heart an adaptation or acceptance of what has been known by the mind and felt about by the emotions.

For us, today, the quiet first phase of love, the receptive acceptance by the heart of what is known by the mind, is neglected. We find it hard to recognise and even to practice. We are too busy. The extent and success of evil upsets us to the core. We feel we have to 'do something immediately'. We are eaten up with desiring, using, possessing things, worrying. A horde of unruly drives and passions has run amok in our heart, in our life, in our society. We need a discipline to still the storm of activist anxiety and craving. Possessiveness and activism have subverted inner calm. We need to develop a practice of meditation or contemplation centred upon falling in love and being in love with the order of being in order to deepen our centre of gravity. We need to set aside enough time on a regular basis to become deep waters that run slow. We need to engage in a sustained practice of attunement to the beauty, order, truth, unity and goodness of being so as to form thereby in our mind and heart the substance of personal order, a right understanding of reality, a right order of loves in the heart, and the right basic dispositions of character to direct us towards right action.

FROM BEING IN LOVE WITH SOME . . .

Whatever we know, we love. No sooner do we know that something exists than we love it, at least a little: then, as we get to know more about that being, we grow to love it more and more. The clearest instance of this for me is being married. On the first few occasions we met, I liked Gemma a little. Then as we got to know one another better, and as we met more frequently and were together for longer, I began to discover what she was really like, her personal qualities and concerns: and as each new excellence came to light I responded to it by an outburst of acceptance. In the delicate interpersonal context of this growth in understanding, then, there occurred those exceptional moments in which in and through something she said or did, a phrase, a tone, a gesture, a spontaneous deed, her innermost self was more revealed, and to that momentary revelation my heart responded with a gentle tidal-wave of acceptance, what is more usually called falling in love. And these moments happen again from time to time, although we cannot summon them up when we wish. Rather, a particular action or expression suddenly intimates the depth, the hidden and sacred depth, that lies at the heart of this person with whom I have lived a dozen years and whom I all too often take for granted as if by now I surely know everything that there is to know about her. These glimpses deepen and renew the falling in love that binds us together and reminds me that this person whom I know better than any other is a mystery even to me who perhaps know her better than anyone else.

As soon as we know anything exists, our heart rests gladly in it; we rejoice in its very being. We are in love with it. This may seem at first glance to be a rather unimportant activity, being in love with this or that: but it hints to us what we are *for* as human persons. As a violin is for playing, so we human persons are for knowing and being in love with being.

And knowing and being in love with some beings brings us some fulfilment. It does not bring us complete fulfilment: as well as the few things we know and love now there are all the other things yet to be known and loved. Nonetheless, this experience shows us that our <u>fulfilment as human persons consists centrally in being in love with</u> <u>what we know</u>. As the bodily drives head towards the objectives in which they find satisfaction, so the human spirit heads naturally and spontaneously towards knowing and loving being as the natural end in which it finds some fulfilment.

. . . TO BEING IN LOVE WITH ALL

If being in love with some beings is what brings us partial fulfilment, what, we may ask, would bring us complete, utter and unending fulfilment? Here indeed is a question to stir imagination, emotions, mind and heart to the depths. The answer that slowly suggests itself to me is this: if knowing and loving some being is what gives us partial fulfilment, then surely knowing and loving all being would give us complete fulfilment. As soon as I formulate this, it is as if a mist ahead of me had cleared momentarily to give me a too-fleeting glimpse of Journey's End. My heart leaps out towards It in a giant step of self-donation so large that it is at once joy and anguish. Home! From the innermost core of my being a white-hot longing flashes, countless light-years deep, a longing which is at once quest and homecoming, reaching and landing. The heart's compass needle finds its North and turns towards it. Surely we would find complete fulfilment in knowing and loving all being, even to the very Ground of being Itself?

Loving Action

A word went down from our hearts to our cities. It came as a lantern to light our way amidst the dark night of depersonalisation. On the road it was set upon by thieves who attacked and wounded it, stripped it of its proper meaning, and left it broken and deformed by misuse by the side of the road. It was not 'they' who did this, but we ourselves. How often have we set upon this word and robbed it of its proper meaning? And how often have we passed by on the other side and refused to turn our heads to see what the trouble was or turn our feet to offer help? But somehow its feeble cry for help never quite leaves our ears: we never quite succeed in extinguishing that within us which urges us to hearken to it, to turn back, to cross over the road, to lift up this broken word and carry it off to an inn of safe-keeping, even to put our hand into our pocket and to pay a penny that the task might be done properly. For it is the word love. And how can we do without love?

We know that our lives should be made up of acts of love, if only we knew what love is and how to do it. We know or at least suspect that what is said or implied about love in the ads and the pop songs, in the chat shows and the magazines, is so shallow as to be useless. But how can we find out for ourselves what love is? In the preceding section we have examined the first phase of love, what we may call the receptive phase; now we have to take a look at the active phase, loving action. By this we mean all the responsible actions that we decide upon and carry out as adults. What are these actions and how should we order them so that they carry forwards the quest of the human person for adequate and proper fulfilment?

THE QUESTION ABOUT LOVING ACTION

The main question about loving action is this: when we perform a free and deliberate action is it truly loving or do we merely suit ourselves? Is human action able to be objective? Can we do what really ought to be done, or only what serves our own interests? Is all the talk about duty, rights, obligations and self-sacrifice nothing more than self-deception to cover up the nastier aspects of our selfishness? Are we so formed that we can only know and do what suits ourselves?

Among the victims of higher education, and even more strongly among its purveyors, the dominant view is that "It is all relative." By this is meant that it is not possible for human beings to go beyond what suits themselves and to discover and do what ought to be done. The level of the discussion is usually rather low: many are content to point out differences between the values, customs and laws of groups who live at different times and places. Tribes in Africa feature frequently. To avoid sinking without a trace in this swamp of opinion and dispute we shall try to follow again the approach that we adopted in the case of knowing.

We shall take a piece of human action from our own experience and examine it from within, so as to identify its elements and to discover how they are fitted together. The drawback in the discussions about social practices in different places is that they remain, for the most part, on the 'outside' of the matter and fail to explore adequately the 'inside', that is, the data of experience. We are able to study responsible action directly because the acts involved are conscious. Here, then, I invite you again to find an instance of yourself engaging in responsible action: examine it and that will enable you to see for yourself. Check my description against your own experience.

What carries us up from the level of 'is' to the level of 'ought' is the little act of receptive acceptance which we examined in the preceding section. Everything we come to know, we love. Now we have to notice how particular 'oughts' begin to emerge from that ever-growing fabric of love for being.

WE ARE GROWING

To understand how we move from merely loving receptively what we know exists, to discovering and doing what ought to be done, we first draw attention to the fact that we are unfinished beings. We are growing, becoming. To check this, ask yourself whether you would be content to remain exactly as you are at this instant. Do you know everything and everyone you want already? Have you done and become all that you wish? Or are there other things you want to know and love and do? Do you regard what you are at this stage as perfect, as complete, or are there improvements that you want to make, parts to be removed and other parts to be added? The fact is that we are beings in process; we are involved in a development that is life-long at least. In addition, we have to observe that we are able to take part in the work of finishing our development: more than that, we have to do so. Human living is so structured that each of us when we become an adult has to take over, to some extent, the running of his or her own life. Human actions do not occur without our making choices and performing deeds: they do not just happen by themselves. So, we are given charge of contributing to our own development. Like the captain of the ship we have to make decisions about where we are going and how we are going to get there: we select the direction and goal that we are going to give to our development, and we select the way, the means, that we are going to follow in order to reach that end. Because we are intelligent we are able to discover that we are imperfect and that we have to participate in our own development: thus, we come to know, as well as the aspects of our being which are, other aspects which are possible and perhaps desirable but which do not yet exist: some of these, we may conclude *ought* to exist, and we ought to take steps to bring them about. it is from our knowing about what is that we understand what does not yet exist, but could be brought about by suitable action, and should be brought about by us.

THE DOER'S DOZEN

Some discussions of this subject begin by constructing the most contorted and complex examples imaginable: I am taking the opposite approach. My example is ordinary, a toothache. Our daughter arrived in one night complaining of a terrible pain in her mouth. This already pushes us further than the kind of experience we have examined in the previous sections of knowing and love, because it is obviously not enough for me to know that this is my daughter and to love her: more is called for than knowing what is the case and accepting it. I have to go beyond knowing what is to working to what ought to be done and then doing it. So, this additional area of human activity, which we have called responsible action, goes beyond knowing and accepting what is, to knowing what ought to be, working out what has to be done in order to bring that about, and then doing that. As in the case of knowing and love, but even more so here, the action is very commonplace and you may find that the parts happen too quickly to distinguish them: if so then you should use a more difficult example, one in which you had to stop and make an effort at different stages: that makes it easier to spot the different parts. And several examples may be required because as soon as the problem becomes routine, then your habitual knowledge and expertise steps in and you do not notice yourself going through the stages because in that example they have been learned previously and now are swiftly re-activated. ∅

The first step is the formation of judgements of value: what the mind knows, the heart loves; but after this act of falling in love with each thing known, the mind again reflects on this and produces a judgement of value: thus, for example, I stand in front of a picture and let it construct in me the experience that it can communicate to me; this evokes in me an act of acceptance and soon afterwards my mind judges "Yes! That is good." So, I know something, then I accept it, then my mind reflects on that acceptance and judges that the thing accepted is good. This last act is a simple judgement of value, and we generate multitudes of such judgements of value as we go along: this is good, that seems good. Or we may judge that this is better than that, or seems so.

In the case of the toothache, I have already made many judgements of value concerning our daughter: the main one is that she is very precious; others include the recognition that her health is important and that it is more important than the uninterruption of my smooth-running daily routine. In response to the reflective clarification of these goods, especially, for example her health, my heart moves from a purely receptive acceptance of them, to an active will that they be realised, a concern or confirmation of them as fitting ends to be pursued if needs be. It may help to schematise this in the form of a list:

Mind.		*Heart.*
1. Judgements of value.	➔	2. Active willing of these goods.

These are, then, the more immediate background to the discovery of the toothache. When we first hear of it, we suspect that it might be a ploy to avoid school, but we are open also to the possibility that it could be a real toothache. Looking is not enough to work out which is the real cause: what is called for is a piece of knowing. This knowing reaches the conclusion that it seems to be a toothache. Once that has been decided I begin to engage in ought-questioning: "What should I do?" The next step is the realisation that something will have to be done to heal this toothache. It is easy to recognise that this realisation is based on the judgements of value already made and on the willing actively to seek those goods, like her health. What it adds to them is the knowledge that a possible good in the area of health is missing and ought to be brought about as soon as possible. We are moving beyond what is to what is possible but not yet achieved. This step is the judgement of value that a healing of her toothache is possible but not yet achieved, and the heart responds to this value judgement by desiring the achievement of that end.

Mind.		*Heart.*
3. Judgement of value. The tootache can be healed: it has not yet been healed: it ought to be healed.	→	4. Intention or desire. I want to bring about this end which is possible but not yet achieved.

The next question is how that desirable end is to be reached. Apart from a feverish midnight search for oil of cloves or a mild pain-killing tablet, the answer that suggests itself is a visit to the dentist. Quickly I work out that I could manage to arrange time off the next morning and so on through all the details. Some have to wait until next morning, the phone call to the surgery to make the appointment, the calls to cancel appointments, but the work of this stage in the process of loving action is clear, it is to work out the set of means that will bring about the desired end.

Mind.		*Heart.*
5. Working out the means. To heal the toothache requires a trip to the dentist which demands these arrangements.	→	6. Consent to the means.

Having worked out the 'how', I am in a position to reach a practical judgement: I ought to do this set of things to reach that end. The core of the reply to those who deny the openness and objectivity of human loving action is an invitation: we have to invite them to pay attention to the presence within themselves of these steps, and especially of this one, the practical judgement. To those who say that morality and ethical living is all relative we reply: Have you ever had this experience of reaching the practical judgement, I know what I should do in that situation here and now? It is from an examination of this experience that the discovery of the openness and objectivity of moral knowing and action arises. Many people are spellbound by words like superego and socialisation and neglect to study moral activity from within by an examination of their own conscious activities. When we do this we discover that what is sometimes ridiculed as the little voice of authority planted within us by our parents and teachers is really our own minds knowing what we ought to do here and now. Conscience means this process of ought-questioning which yields the practical judgement, I ought to do this here and now. It is a commonplace experience, this reaching of practical judgements; and it is equally a commonplace that many of them are clearly objective and some are clearly wrong. But we are often able to tell the difference. For example, a young mother who tries to feed her newly born infant chocolate because she saw on an ad that there is milk in it, is making a mistake, but it is not impossible to discover that. But who is ready to stand up and say either that they never make any practical judgements whatever, or that none of their practical judgements are right, or that they are totally unable to discover whether any of their practical judgements are right?

The heart responds to the practical judgement by the free choice either to act according to the practical judgement or not to do so. There is much confusion about the meaning of the word freedom and many deny that human beings are free. Some are so horrified by the ways some people dominate and restrict others that they are just too impassioned to consider any other meaning of freedom than the absence of external coercion. Others are impressed by the fact that in a group people tend to act similarly and are led to deny freedom. What we are doing is analysing a piece of human action in order to identify and understand its parts. The parts we are examining here are the practical judgement and the heart's response to it. This is an empirical question: how, in fact, does the heart respond to practical judgements? The answer is to be found by adverting to one's own conscious experience. In fact, when we have worked out what we ought to do, then we experience within ourselves that we are able either to do what we know we ought to do, or not to do it: and this indeterminacy of the heart with respect to the direction of the mind is what is meant by human freedom. It does not mean that the mind gives no direction and that leaves the heart free. No, the mind points out what ought to be done, but the heart is still not thereby compelled to do that; it may, or it may not. Thus, the heart's response to the practical judgement is choice. This poses a problem only because the moral knowledge is objective and is quite likely to come up with a course of action that does not suit us at all, that involves us, in fact, in inconvenience, risk, discomfort, or even suffering! Because the practical judgement is likely to demand of us something we do not want to do, we have moral dilemmas and agonise over them.

Mind.   *Heart.*
7. Practical judgement. ➔ 8. Free Choice.
  I ought to do this.   I will / I will not do this.

The matter, of course, does not rest here. The mind responds to the free choice by ordering me to go ahead and implement my choice if it is right or prohibiting it if I have chosen against following the practical judgement. It is this act of self-command in which the mind directs the heart towards right action which is often called the voice of conscience. The heart responds to its prescription by action: the practical judgement is either implemented or not.

Mind.   *Heart.*
 9. Self-command. ➔ 10. Action.
   Do it!   I do it.

So the necessary arrangements are made and next morning we set off to the dentist. Ingrid's grandfather was a dentist, so she wants to drop into the Church on the way to have a word with him about the approaching ordeal. She is frightened but brave. Throughout the session she keeps a tight grip on my finger. I do my best to appear outwardly calm. I look out the window and watch a bird wandering in and out of a clump of grass against the wall. I hear the dentist trying to speak reasonably about the desirability of her releasing his finger from between her teeth. he massages his mangled finger and lies, "You were very good, my dear". The tears are wiped away: hers, I mean. A shocked Ingrid explores her numb jaw and, I suppose, wonders why on earth she should have to say thank you to the person who inflicted all this on her. She stumbles into the car muttering darkly about never again eating chocolate and washing her teeth regularly from now on. Soon, however, she begins to brighten up and tries to discover whether I still believe in the Tooth Fairy, and whether there is any chance that he/she/it might be persuaded to leave anything for fillings bravely endured. She prepares to enjoy her brief role as the wounded heroine returning from the wars. Over the next couple of days we watch for signs of gangrene, haemorrage, or any of the other possible ill-effects that inhabit the imaginations of parents. Eventually, I conclude that everything is satisfactory. She is well again. My heart relaxes in the knowledge of a job well done: and I keep half an eye open for the signs that the next disaster has arrived.

Mind.	Heart.
11. Judgement of completion. →	12. Enjoyment of the end reached,
Well, that is finished.	and relaxation.

The dominant opinion today is that objectivity is impossible to reach in human moral judgement and action. I cannot agree. When I analyse my own experience I find many instances in which I discover and do what should be done. Take the case of the toothache: my moral judgement was that she should go to the dentist. Was that a purely subjective view? Of course not! Was it objective? Well, she had a severe pain: it was apparently in her tooth: we went to the dentist and he said that there was indeed tooth decay and he removed it and filled the tooth. And the pain stopped. If that is not objective, I don't know what is. Did its correctness as a piece of knowing or action depend solely on what was inside me? Not at all! My knowing reached out to discover what really was the problem and what really should be done, and my heart saw to it that it was done. The knowing was objective and the action was right. How can you deny this without playing with words or ceasing to engage in reasonable and responsible discussion? We meet these moral situations every day. Are all our actions private fancies totally disconnected from what is really happening and what needs to be done? To be sure, there are many cases which are much more complicated. The knowing can be mistaken because of ignorance or error, because of a lack of a mature experience of life, or because of a resistance to reality grounded in emotional suffering. The knowing can be deformed by rationalisation in which we attempt to deny, conceal, excuse or misinterpret our failure to do what we knew we should have done, but chose not to do. It can be deformed also due to spiritual resistance to the order of being and by ideology. And even where the knowing is intact the doing may not follow because it would involve suffering or inconvenience. There are, also, situations in which we are torn between fairly evenly matched goods and hesitate to choose between them, and situations in which the difficulty of evaluating the consequences of the various possible courses of action is compounded by the fact that we have to make a decision within a certain time limit. None of these additional complications, however, prove that we are unable to reach objective concrete practical judgements, or that we are unable to do what we know we ought to do: all they show is that in many cases objective moral judgement and right action are difficult.

As in the case of our examination of knowing, we usually do not identify all the elements by studying a single example: where we have already mastered that sort of situation, the elements of knowing and willing involved have become habitual and occur without effort, so it is difficult to appreciate where they fit in and what part they play in the whole process. Several examples are needed.

In this outline of the process involved in responsible action it is important to recall that the object of such action is a particular end or objective which we understand to be possible, worthwhile but not yet achieved. We call this process loving action to emphasise the fact that it rests upon an already achieved fabric of knowledge and love of being: this knowledge and love places us in a position to notice a disorder that needs to be corrected or an additional excellence that could and should be introduced. In other words, it is being, known and loved, that is the principle and spring of the process of responsible action. And as the heart's receptive acceptance of known being is the source of the process, so too, it is its end. The final pair of steps in the doer's dozen, what we call the judgement of completion and the enjoyment and resting in, are a knowing of the new good that our action has brought about and a loving of it.

Here, then, is the other dimension that is in us but not in the animals:

■ There is a drive in us that underlies and pushes ahead the different kinds of acts that we spontaneously perform after we have known: the falling and being in love, and the process of responsible action. This drive carries us on from the knowing to the love and on to the responsible action.

■This drive is conscious once awakened. We experience it as a desire. I experience also, that it is the same I who loves and acts responsibly as sees and hears, moves and feels, eats and sleeps, and knows.

■This desire is a desire to love the being we know and to discover and do what ought to be done.

■This desire is a desire to love the being we know in its excellence, and to discover and bring about by our free action the correction of defects in being, or the introduction of additional excellences in being which are possible and worthwhile but not yet achieved.

Here, we have to say, we have discovered the other capacity of the human spirit: as well as its capacity to animate the human body and ground the operations of sensitive consciousness, such as seeing, and its capacity to understand, we have to recognise the existence of the capacity to love being as good, and to know and do freely what ought to be done.

THE SEARCH FOR THE RIGHT ORDER OF HUMAN EXISTENCE

As an overall symbol for the exploration undertaken in this book I chose 'the journey': we find, now, that the journey of personal exploration is only part of the wider quest which is our life as a whole. We are radically unfinished beings called upon to take part in our own completion: called upon, also, to work out for ourselves, to some extent, what we are and what we are for, and on that basis, to order our lives so as to bring us towards what we found to be our purpose. Human life is a search for the right order of human existence. We have to find out what we are and what we are for, and then to work out how we ought to live so as to move towards what we should be achieving.

Human existence has several dimensions. At the core there is the human person and the personal area of existence. But we live in groups, in the family, in the neighbourhood, in a society among other societies, in the flow of history over time. During history individuals and groups develop different views about the nature and purpose of the human person and how we should live, so there is the further dimension of the meetings and interactions between these views and their proponents, which constitutes the historical dimension of existence. lastly, we live in the world which has an order of its own and we have to work out how we should relate to it.

The need for a special 'journey' at this time is due, in part, to the fact that in our day and for some time previously, Western civilization has been undergoing an acute loss or deformation of the traditional store of insight into the human spirit. The loss and deformation are at least centuries deep and planetwide. Their results are swift and awful. We no longer understand what we are or what we are for, so we no longer know how we should live. The ways of living we devise fail to satisfy us because they cannot bring us towards what we are meant to reach. Instead, they wreak havoc in our personal lives, in society, in history and in the world.

By our loving action we shape the world around us in an obvious way, and we influence and affect the people around us, perhaps in a less dramatic way. But we also shape ourselves, we make ourselves into this or that kind of person. Whatever we do over and over again becomes habitual to us, easy to repeat but hard to go against: and all our habits of thinking, feeling and acting fit together in a more or less coherent order which is our character. As we have seen, the first phase of love, the receptive acceptance of the various things we meet, poses few difficulties: the problems begin to arise when we have to act. Then we have to work out which things are better than others and what order of priorities we should have regarding them. An additional problem arises because of the fact that we start off knowing and loving nothing and slowly get to know and love one thing after another, and while we are doing this as children, we are taught and formed by the older generation, by our parents and neighbours, our teachers and leaders, and generally by our society. We are shaped so as to have a particular scale of preferences before we are mature enough to know whether that scale of preferences is right or wrong. Then, when we reach adolescence and early adulthood we begin to realise that from here on it is up to each one of us to decide for himself or herself whether we are going to accept that scale of preferences as a whole, or whether we are going to add new parts and remove some bits, or even make a radical change in the system of values which we have been formed to follow. What drives us to take this problem seriously is the fact that we realise that in and through the action that we do, we are shaping the kind of person we become. If we find that the prospect of becoming like some or most of the people in our society appals us, then we are moved to give urgent attention to the question of discovering a different scale of preferences which will lead us to shape ourselves in another way. Our actions, thus, have a playful and a serious dimension. Insofar as a particular deed concerns matters which are of limited and not-necessary importance, we have a certain detachment from them: but insofar as in and through those actions we are shaping our own character, they have a deadly seriousness.

Since we begin to exist at a certain point and have to learn what we are and how we ought to act so as to reach proper development and fulfilment, we are in the hands of the older generation for most of the first two decades of our life. The turning point comes when we realise that as adults it is up to us to decide what we do and what scale of preferences we are going to follow. One of the most important decisions at that point is our decision to become adequately self-directing. My actions are shaping me: therefore, from now on, I am going to try to be as clear as I can about what direction my actions are leading me, and I am going to try to choose my actions so that they carry me where I decide to go. This is the responsibility of adulthood.

This time of decision has two dimensions. We ask whether we are living in such a way as to be and grow in accordance with our ideals, our principles, the things we put first in our lives: in other words, we measure our habits of action and our routines, our whole way of living against what we hold to be the right order of human existence. Am I living the way my view of the human person demands? A second more disturbing dimension arises when we realise that there are many traditions about the human person and how we ought to live. Is ours the right one? Or are there others more adequate to the kind of being we find ourselves to be? Should we add elements from other traditions to our own? Should some elements of our tradition be removed as mistakes or corruptions of the real tradition? The journey in which we are engaged in these pages is intended to raise this second range of questions. It has been my discovery that the view of the human person which is dominant in Western civilization today is largely false and corrupt, and that the way of living based on it damages us.

From the experience of being dissatisfied and damaged by the dominant view of the human person arose a journey in search of the truth about the human person. Now that journey has reached the discovery of self-direction: we ought to be directing our own development. This insight raises the central question: to speak of direction is to think of heading towards something, but towards what are we meant to be moving as human persons? What should the goal of human development be? What should we be making of ourselves? The line of inquiry that I am following is quite easily expressed: what we are should give us an indication of what we are for, an idea of how we should live so as to reach that end. What we are determines what we are for, and what we are for determines how we should live so as to achieve our purpose. It is certainly not meant to be an original idea: I got it from Plato and Aristotle, Augustine and Thomas, Lonergan and Voegelin, and I accept it because it makes more sense of my experience and life than any of the many other answers I have met and examined. It fits what I find myself to be.

LONG NIGHT'S JOURNEY INTO DAY

What are we? We are human persons. We have a beginning to our existence when we know and love nothing. As we go along we come to know and love one thing after another. We are on a journey from the pitch-black darkness of knowing and loving nothing, through a dark night and slowly dawning morning of knowing and loving ever more and more, until at long last we stumble among the clouds of unknowing and unlove to reach the blinding, blazing, bright-burning brilliance of high-noon daylight, knowing and loving all, and above all, the Sun by Whose light we know and love all else.

Earth's Centre

The Earth's journey seems to have no end:
In circles see her run.
In truth, however, she plays around her home:
Her centre is the Sun.

CHAPTER 4

JOURNEY'S END

We began from the question of identity, Who am I? The recognition that each of us is a mystery grew from a consideration of the question, Is there more to me than meets the eye? A symbolic attempt to give an account of the hidden dimension of the human person led us to characterise it as person-depth. The realisation that there is such an inner dimension to us drew our attention to the fact that in our society awareness of that interior area of the person has, by and large, been lost, and that the vocabulary required to articulate it has also been lost. The next step was to go beyond the symbolic imagery of depth and to face the question, What makes me more than an animal? This led to an analysis of our knowing, our loving and our responsible action. We found that as well as the body with a sensitive consciousness similar to that of some of the higher animals, there is also in each of us a human spirit with the capacity to know, love and act freely and responsibly.

We noticed, then, that in and through our responsible activity we shape not only the world and the people around us, but also the development of our own character and that brings us to our final question, What am I for? We realise that the mark of adulthood is the achievement of independence and autonomy in which we become self-directing: we choose what to make of ourselves. But what are we to make of ourselves? In what direction are we to shape our development? Surely, if we are to point ourselves in the right direction we need to know what we are for: otherwise how are we to select the right direction? That brings us to our present question: what is the proper and natural end of the human person? What is a human being meant to move towards? What am I for?

Our society offers several answers to this question. Indeed, it does more than offer answers; by compelling us to participate in an educational system largely determined by the state and by surrounding us with mass media and public opinion, it virtually imposes upon us its own lifestyle and the purpose of personhood implicit in it. If we try to examine what society holds to be the purpose of the individual we usually find it to be rather confused and incoherent, but it is our participation in the life of that society which is the greatest single external force shaping the way we think and feel, act and choose. Societies vary in the degree to which they permit any deviation from a dominant pattern: in some societies, we are allowed to meet many different lifestyles: others try to restrict its members' contacts with alternatives. We noted that there were two moments in the process by which the individual takes up his or her attitude to a way of life proposed by society: firstly we ask whether our conduct is in tune with the view offered by society, or by our tradition within the society; a more radical critique begins when we ask whether the ways of living actually found in the society are themselves authentic embodiments of those traditions, or whether corruptions have crept in and unwanted elements have been dropped. The journey to the Centre of the person undertaken in these pages arose from an inquiry of the second sort and from the discovery that the lifestyles offered by the society and the views of the human person dominant in the society do not correspond to what I find in my own experience. Clearly the society around is in a mess: now I find that its understanding of the human person is radically inadequate and incomplete; surely these two facts are related. The conclusion suggests itself that the social disorder is the result of the mass-implementation of an incorrect view of what a human being is.

When we begin to question the 'received opinion' on what we are and what we are for, we run into resistance from society. When we challenge the generally held opinion we are told "But everyone knows that this is so." A tyranny of fashion or habit obstructs unwanted questioning. There is also an inertia, a mental laziness that makes most people follow the crowd in what they think. Again, the basic presuppositions of the dominant way of life are rarely put into words and examined carefully: they are taken for granted. They are like the spectacles through which we see reality, rather than a part of reality that needs to be examined critically and understood correctly. There is a climate of opinion which knits a whole set of opinions together so that to question one is to be seen to threaten the whole:

and that threat is met by ridicule or disinterest. In a climate of opinion, incorrect views about the nature of the human person are like pollution. Precisely because the views are incorrect there is an anxiety whenever they are questioned. The way we live is corrupt because a multitude of injustices form the basis of our material comfort; to take the most obvious example, the affluence of the developed Northern part of the planet rests on its exploitation of the South. Whoever would bring the truth to light would raise the unwanted question of reordering the planetary economy in accordance with justice, and for this reason certain lines of inquiry are discouraged. This is accomplished by what we may call 'talker terrorism', that is, putting someone down aggressively when they ask unwanted questions. There are many styles of talker terrorism but the most effective are ridicule, ignoring the questions and pretending that such questions can be dismissed because they are not 'scientific'. Whenever we feel ourselves under attack for asking certain questions we can be sure that we have run into a talker terrorist. At that moment we should recall that the unfolding of an inquiry by the raising of questions is the natural activity of the human spirit.

To violate the inbuilt thrust of the human spirit by the wrongful suppression of inquiry injures both the suppressor and the suppressed. Each experiences an anxiety, an unease. The way to heal the wound of mindache is simply to begin to follow the line of inquiry, to resist the interference in the unfolding of our questioning, to raise the forbidden questions.

Behind such interference, suppression and prohibition of questioning lies its motivation. This motivation is usually the desire not to have to face certain facts about the way we are living. When the way we are living does not accord with what we are, then we experience a deep dissatisfaction. When we dread the radical reformation of our lifestyle which we sense would be demanded by a clear facing of the facts, then we take the easy way out and try to block the emergence of the facts by hindering our knowing from proper development. The disproportion between the way we live and what we really are causes in us a heartache, a pulsing experience of wrongness which we try to blot out by engaging in various intense types of experience.

In our day, the widespread loss of awareness of the human spirit and its nature, the general incomprehension of what it is and how it should develop, has produced in us an acceptance of the resulting spiritual disorder as normal: mindache and heartache are taken for granted as natural rather than recognised as symptoms of an epidemic. Because many people have no way to still the mindache and heartache that rage within them, they have nothing to compare them to, and so they cannot grasp that they are a spiritual disorder.

What sparked off the journey to the Centre of the person presented in these pages was the idea that the whole view of the human being that underlies modernity might be wrong: and during the last fifteen years my suspicion has been confirmed. The modern way of viewing the human being takes it for granted that there is not in us a human spirit. Or if lipservice is still paid to the idea of the human spirit, there is no real personal understanding of the words. The whole way our society is organised implies the view of the person as closed, as a non-spiritual thing. To clarify the extent to which the open understanding of the human being challenges the closed view we ask the question, What am I for?

There are many ways to go about answering this question, but there seem to be only six types of answer. When I ask, What am I for? I may answer:

1. I don't care.
2. I am for society.
3. I am for myself.
4. I am not for any of the things in the world, in particular.
5. I am not for anything at all.
6. I am for nothing on earth, but rather for Something out of this world.

1. I DON'T CARE

You do not have to go far on the journey to the Centre of the person to learn that when you ask people such searching questions many of them feel threatened by them and answer, I don't care. They say that they are too practical, too busy, to have time for such abstract theoretical questions. This answer is partly true: it is quite obvious that they do keep themselves very busy from morning till night. We live in an activist society in which we are encouraged to do, to work, to consume, to possess. We work by day and we sleep by night: whatever time, money and energy we have left over we tend to spend on entertaining ourselves. We never have a moment to stop. We never take time to pause and ask where we are going with all our busy-ness. Eat, drink and have fun, we believe, for tomorrow we die. If we do take this time off to examine the way we live, we discover that for all the talk and activity directed to happiness, there is very little of that precious element about. Who is happy? Are you? True, we have our moments, but that is all they are, moments: and like bubbles they burst. When we do take a few moments off to ask whether all our vigorous and frenzied doing is really making us happy, we discover that we are not really happy. It crosses our mind that the very intensity of our doing is suspicious: it looks very much as if we are deliberately keeping ourselves busy so that we never have to face the howl of mindache and heartache, and the terror of the question, What is the point of it all? Where is all my activity leading? Why bother? Slowly we realise that the busy-ness of modernity is primarily a ploy to conceal from ourselves our dread in the face of the mystery of our finality as human persons. We say, I don't care, but we make sure to cram our day and night with an excess of activity in order to avoid having to face these questions. But do not believe me: check for yourself. Do you experience in yourself any resistance to taking the time to face this ultimate question about your personal destiny? What are you for? How do you respond to that question. Ask others the same question. Do you notice an anxious aggressiveness in their disclaimers? Are they securely happy? If they are securely at ease and happy, then why the aggressiveness when that question is posed?

2. I AM FOR SOCIETY

One of the strongest experiences that pushed me to undertake this exploration of the person was the revulsion I felt when I met ideologies that said I am nothing more than a part of some totalitarian whole and that by taking part in it I would find fulfilment. Something central in me said no to anything that would reduce me to an instrument for others to use, or to a part in some social machine. Today there are many such ideologies: they claim that the person is for the state, the class, the race, the business company, the party, the society. Others see us as just another animal species and say that the individual is for the species. These views have a grain of truth in them as far as they go. A society is an order to provide the goods that its members need. The society is for its members. If we say that we are for society, we still leave the question unanswered because what goods society provides depends upon the view of the human person held by its ruling groups. One truth in that view is that each of these groups has a role to play in the common life and that we have responsibilities towards many of these groups. The other truth in these views is that the human person does not blossom alone but within community. But the difference between a community and a totalitarian group is precisely that the community recognises and respects the spiritual nature and demands of the person and provides the conditions for its flowering, whereas a totalitarian group denies and suppresses the human spirit. It is only as we begin to regain some sensitivity to the nature and demands of the human spirit that we appreciate that society cannot be the natural and final end of the person: it cannot bring us total and final fulfilment. Again, the rediscovery of the human spirit helps us to be clear about what it is in us that is not in the animals: the presence of this additional dimension means that we are not an animal species. To regard the person as primarily an instrument for others to use, or as a piece in a social machine is to disregard the nature and finality of the human spirit.

3. I AM FOR MYSELF

The foundation stone of the closed view of the person that dominates Western civilization today is the opinion that I am for myself. It is from the excesses produced by this opinion that militant totalitarian collectivism has grown. Are we for ourselves? Am I for myself? As with the previous answer, there is a grain of truth in this opinion. It is obvious that when we resist the totalitarian claim of the party, the race, the class, the state or the species, we are asserting the primacy of the person over the society. When we try to work out exactly what we mean by saying that each one is for himself or herself, we run into several knotty problems. The question is, What is the human person for? We may begin by recognising that each person happens to have certain likes and dislikes, and certain talents. Do we mean that each one is for these? One man collects stamps, another enjoys hurting people: do we say, "Each to his own preference!"? Are there limits to what each one may do in the pursuit of what he fancies? How are such limits to be decided? By power? Is might right? The question to be faced here is, What does the other person mean to me? If each person is primarily for himself or herself, then how should we treat one another? If the other person stands between me and something that I want, what should I do? If I can get something I desire by exploiting other people, why shouldn't I do so? The answers to these questions hinge upon what we consider to be the purpose of the human person. If the human individual has no further purpose than the satisfaction of his own desires, then why should he care if others get hurt in the process? If hurting others displeases him he may choose to refrain from it to increase his comfort: or if there is a law-enforcement agency he may refrain from hurting others to avoid the risk of punishment; but when it comes down to brass tacks, the final standard that decides what is to be done is his own arbitrary preference. Is that the way you see it? This ugly picture is what follows once we accept that each person is primarily for himself. But the question we have to answer is not whether we like the picture, but whether it is true. It is the dominant view in contemporary Western civilization: dominant groups acting on this view have made the world what it is today. If that view is wrong, then we have found a starting point for envisioning a new social order. The first point that has to be made about this view is that it is based upon an incorrect understanding of the human spirit. It presumes that human knowing, loving and responsible action are closed, that we are unable to go beyond what suits us to know, love and do what ought to be done. But we have found that the human spirit is open, that we do go beyond what we like to what is, what is good, what ought to be done. It is only because the human mind does transcend selfish preference that we are able to recognise the existence of selfishness at all: if our minds were unable to know the difference between what we want and what we should do, we would never conceive of such a thing as selfishness as a personal disorder. We would regard meanness and cruelty as natural to man. Do you? In fact, the human mind goes beyond what suits or pleases me to judge what is the case, and what ought to be done, whether or not it suits me. More technically, we have to note that when we examined our knowing we found that it only works when there are things there to be known: and that our loving and action, too, presuppose the existence and nearness of things to be loved and perfected. Concretely, then, it seems that we have to say that the spiritual part of us, as much as the bodily part, is for activities that regard beings other than itself, and that in and through these activities of knowing, loving and perfecting these beings, it moves towards its own proper perfection. What this means, however, is that the answer, I am for myself! does not really answer the question, What am I for? We have to persist in the inquiry and ask further questions. Certainly, we accept that each person in some sense exists for himself or herself, insofar as the purpose of our existence is to be as fully as we can. As a general answer this is true. But it does not tell us how to live. It does not tell us what direction to point the development of our character that is taking place through our responsible activities. What we want to know is what exactly we ought to be doing in order to move towards our natural and proper fulfilment. The reply that the proper purpose or end of man is the rightly ordered activity of his capacities is only generic: we want to fill it out concretely. We want to discover what precisely constitutes rightly ordered activity of our human capacities.

4. I AM NOT FOR ANY OF THE THINGS IN THE WORLD, IN PARTICULAR

We have discovered within us as our distinguishing feature, the human spirit with capacities to know and love being. As human persons we are radically open, that is, we are able to know and love whatever crosses our path. When we ask, What are we for? an answer that springs to mind is that we are for knowing and loving and perfecting whatever crosses our path. Like the other answers encountered so far, this one also has its grain of truth: it is true as far as it goes. We do know and love what we meet, and in our responsible activity we heal or perfect the people and things around us and also ourselves. However, it was precisely that fact which led us to the further question as to the goal of all this change; where should we be heading? In what direction should we be steering our knowing, loving and personal development? Is this the only meaning to human existence, to know and love one thing or person after another until we die?

The truth in this view is that we are open: we can and do know and love whatever we meet. This view becomes untrue if it claims to be the end of the inquiry, if we conclude that there is nothing more to be said. The further insight to be gained is the hugeness of the human mind and heart. We are radically open: from the ability to know and love whatever we meet, we grasp the fact that the human spirit is wider than any of the things in the world. There is no single being in the world about which we have to say, I am for this! In fact, we need a mixture of things to live, some food and drink, some air and light, and so on. And we are woven into a human fabric made up of many people, parents and children, in-laws and relations, neighbours and officials, friends and acquaintances. Most of these are not in our lives by our choice entirely. In one sense, the human condition is such that it places us in relationships with people and we have to make the best of them. But before them all we discover that we are free because none of them, and no combination of them, strikes us as necessarily our full and final perfection and fulfilment. True, the universe is filled to overflowing with beautiful and marvellous beings each of which delights us and brings a spark of partial fulfilment to the human spirit. But it is also true to say that even this profusion fails to sate the hunger of the human spirit. It serves, rather, to whet our appetite for more. The delight of the mind and heart in the exuberant multiplicity of beings is not a perfect and lasting fulfilment. It offers, instead, the repeated experience of the human spirit outstripping each and all of these. From this we discover that the adequate range of the human spirit is wider than any or all of these partial fulfilments. We do know and love the particular things and people in the world, but we know also that none of them, nor any combination of them, constitutes our proper and necesary final end. They are not what we are for; we are for more. Nothing in the world, we are driven to recognise, is immense enough to fill and still the quest of human personhood for ever and fully. Nothing in the world is immense enough to match the range and depth of the mind's and heart's longing. They are simply not the right size or kind.

The nearest we come in the world to something that satisfies the human person is friendship. Yet even the most intense form of friendship, marriage, teaches us in depth and detail that we are not enough for one another. The shared understanding and love of marriage's lifelong friendship salts the thirst of the human spirit for participation in huger interpersonal communion. Marriage persuades us that we are emptinesses in search of understanding and love without end or limit: can two emptinesses fill one another?

5. I AM NOT FOR ANYTHING AT ALL

I have tried to arrange the answers to the question, What am I for? in such a way that they lead on from one to the next in an order of increasing depth, much as we might discover them if we were to begin the inquiry for the first time. In fact when we meet people, life has already pushed some of them through the earlier, more superficial answers. I am utterly convinced that if we remain true to the spirit of inquiry and face the full range of our own experiences we cannot stop at any of the earlier answers: at least if we do stop, then we do so not for a good reason, but because something is preventing us from following the flow of the inquiry; and that something, as we have said, is, usually, either a personal wound or else a pressure from the climate of opinion which desires not to face some aspect of the dominant way of living.

We noticed already that in human living there is an interplay of seriousness and detachment: the task at hand may be trivial in itself and so we feel quite detached from it; however, in and through that little task, we are shaping the development of our character in the one and only life we have, and that lends a seriousness to it. Now, it becomes clear that this interplay is related to the fact that we are notr for any of the things in the world, in particular. Now, as we come to the end of this inquiry, the awful importance of this question becomes clear that this interplay is related to the fact that we are not are not any of the things in the world! When we discover this for ourselves, rather than just reading it as someone else's conclusion, it sends a chill running along the spine. We realise that we are touching upon something which our way of life has taught us to ignore because it has no adequate account of its meaning. Here is something uncomfortable and disturbing, something we would rather not face. But life forces us to face the facts, even if we refuse to follow up their meaning. We are born, live for a few years and die. What does it mean? So much suffering and effort goes into every life only to be cut short at random by accident, illness, terrorist attack or war. What's the point, then? We lavish love and care on a child only to watch him go wrong and do evil? Why does it happen? We spend so much time and money on health, paying minute care to our diet and exercise, only to be told that we have cancer. What is the point of doing anything in this life when we know that our efforts may be cut short against our will by factors beyond our control? We search to find and adopt a way of life that does not involve hurting and using other people, only to see those with no such qualms enjoy the fruits of worldly success and prosperity. Why should we bother to make the effort to live a just life when the wicked prosper? Why do the innocent suffer? We have spent years trying to discover what we are, in order to be able to live in accordance with our humanity: but why bother? What is the point, when in the end we die? What is the meaning or purpose, the value or worth of our life when in the end it all comes to dust? This is a valid question. We have all asked it personally at one time or another: life squeezes it out of us sooner or later. In the dead of the night we lie awake in terror at the thought that one day, all the things we are so attached to, all the things we have spent our days building up, these will all die: in that moment we understand that unless we are for Something out of this world, then we are for nothing, nothing at all.

Today we are transfixed by this question: our whole culture is stunned by a panic at the prospect of death and suffering, moral evil and failure. Because we have lost sight of the human spirit, because we no longer know what we are as human persons and consequently how we ought to live so as to unfold that spirit properly, these negative parts of human life have become a million times more terrifying to us. Because we have become blind to the full range of the human spirit, we have convinced ourselves that we *must* be able to find our proper fulfilment in the things in the world. We do not believe that there are any other things so we *have* to believe that we can find fulfilment in the things in the world. It is this which has driven us with such anguished desperation to ask too much of the things in the world. We are paralysed and panic-stricken by the dread that there may be nothing at all that can give us full and final fulfilment, that we are mistakes, cosmic misfits, that we do not fit into the universe. The anxiety that this thought releases within us causes us to fix our attention on this or that thing or person in the world and to try to make it give us full and final satisfaction. It does not work: it cannot work. We are simply not made that way.

In these pages I have quoted only one book, *The Myth of Sisyphus* by Albert Camus: I quoted him because he is one of the few thinkers of our time who have faced this critical issue fully and explored it in depth. He believed, when he wrote the book, that the human person is not for anything in particular. He explored the human person in depth and discovered the infiniteness of the human longing for intelligibility, unity, meaning and goodness. He recognised that nothing in the world was immense enough to match the size of that human longing. He was unable to find Something utterly and unlimitedly understanding and loving. He drew the hard conclusion that human beings in the universe are an absurdity; we do not fit, we are too big for the world, our longing for meaning and value can find nothing in the world that is big enough to satisfy it. The closedness of the mind and heart to the existence of things beyond the world is what characterises this kind of modern consciousness: we find ourselves closed to the possibility that there is Something out of this world, Whose immensity would match the thrust of the human spirit, Whose infinite actuality would fulfil in a full, final and everlasting way the infinite potentiality of the human capacity to know and love. With extraordinary precision Camus recognises this modern closure as a defect, a distortion, a disease of the spirit. "There will be found here", he writes in the opening page, "merely the description, in the pure state, of an intellectual malady." And in a Preface written over a dozen years later he says that in the book he was trying to discover whether human life has a meaning, and to do so from the viewpoint that had become dominant in Western civilization at the time of writing, that is to say, a worldview "without the aid of eternal values which, temporarily perhaps, are absent or distorted in contemporary Europe." Here Camus is recognising that the modern closedness of consciousness to the existence of Something out of this world which provides the ultimate meaning to human existence, that closure is an intellectual disease, a spiritual illness, a disorder of the mind and heart.

It is at this point that the understanding of the human person that grows out of our exploration of the human spirit is likely to break most sharply with the closed view that is dominant in Western society today. Because we have paid close attention to the human spirit in its characteristic operations of knowing, loving and free responsible loving action, we have discovered the real openness of the human spirit: we are a pure capacity to know and love being, and that spiritual capacity is not, and cannot be satisfied by knowing and loving any of the things in the world. It is simply too big and they are just too small. The viewpoint that predominates in Western civilization today says that there is nothing else apart from the world, and that, therefore, unless we are for the things in the world, we are for nothing at all. Or rather, to be more accurate, we are so terrified out of our wits by this whole issue that we try to suppress such questions altogether by feverish attempts to find ultimate satisfaction in some of the things in the world. This is our form of despair, to pretend that the finite things in the world are infinite and are able to match the reach of the human spirit. We agree, then, that we are not for any of the things in the world, insofar as what is meant is that while these things are good and are appropriate for us in many ways, still no one of them nor any combination of them forces us to recognise it as necessarily our proper and natural end; and as a matter of experience, nothing in the world is able to bring us full and final fulfilment. We cannot agree, however, that we are for nothing at all because that further conclusion rests on two presuppositions which we have found to be incorrect.

6. I AM FOR NOTHING ON EARTH, BUT RATHER FOR SOMETHING OUT OF THIS WORLD

Those who claim that we are for nothing at all, that there is no specific reality which is the natural and proper end of the human person, base this claim on two related mistakes, a mistaken view of what human knowing is, and a mistaken view about what human knowing can reach. It is becoming clearer as our exploration of mind and heart advances that the whole view of the human person upon which modern Western civilization is built is radically defective because of its inaccuracy and ignorance about the nature of the human spirit. An imaginative rather than an empirical and analytic account of knowing leads many to deny firstly, that the human capacity to know and love being is infinite in potentiality, and secondly, that the human mind can and does discover the existence of Something other than the things in the world. The fact that both of these conclusions are so tied to the mistaken view of the human mind encourages us to explore the possibility that our recovery of the nature of the human spirit will lead to a more adequate understanding of the ultimate finality of the human person.

One of the most exciting memories I have of the books I read as a child is the great moment in *Robinson Crusoe* when the hero first comes upon the human footprints in the sand! When he saw the marks he understood that they were not just some chance scratches but a human footprint: he understood also that the marks had not made themselves: something had made them. This kind of understanding is commonplace: when we see tracks we ask questions about them. These tracks are what we called earlier, mysteries. A mystery is something which is there, which we can sense in some way; we are aware that it is present; it has a meaning; we are aware that it has a meaning; we do not yet know what that meaning is; we are aware that we do not yet know what the meaning is; and we are attracted by the meaning that lies beyond our grasp. A track is like this; it is something we sense; we understand that it has a meaning; we grasp part of the meaning; we understand that there is further meaning that we do not yet grasp; we are attracted by that further meaning. The sight of the footprint sparks off the understanding that it is a footprint rather than a random mark: that understanding also recognises that beyond the track lies that which left the track: where there's a footprint, there's a foot! This jump of understanding from the track to the track-maker is not a metaphorical or imaginative jump; it is an act of understanding. We may describe its content by saying that in this kind of insight we grasp that the sense-data are partially self-explanatory, and partially not self-explanatory: in other words, the footprint has enough order about it for us to understand that it is not just a chance mark in the sand, but a footprint: but we understand also that more has to be said about the mark; it had to be made by a foot: then the understanding that it is a footprint sets off the discovery that a foot must have made it. When we see tracks we are drawn to ask questions about what made them: when we see tracks we understand that they are not without explanation because there is order and intelligibility in them and we understand that their explanation is not within them but beyond them.

When we were trying to express the openness and the transcendent reach of the human spirit we found Camus' words helpful: he recognised in the human being a desire for unlimited understanding, unity, love and goodness. He saw that we are too big for the world; our spiritual capacities reach beyond the world. Each of us, then, is a Jack-in-the-box, a Jill-in-the-box, an open thirst for being which drives us to know and to love. As we appropriate this more adequate vision of human personhood our mind and heart leap out through the roof of the world and spring beyond the world in hot pursuit of broader being! The multitude of things and people that we meet and come to know and love act like salt on the spiritual thirst which is the deepest core of our personhood: they whet and awaken our appetite for more. The knowledge and love of them works within us like the magic beans in the story, and from them sprouts forth an amazing beanstalk which reaches skywards up through the clouds and out of this world! And we suspect that if only we climb that beanstalk we will reach our heart's desire.

But we perform this leap out of the world, not in any imaginary physical jump, nor in a purely metaphorical sense, nor in some occult elitist experience, but simply by doing a piece of knowing and loving like those we examined earlier.

In this piece of knowing and loving we take a giant step out of this world. Like any other piece of knowing, this one begins when we ask questions about certain things in the world that we experience. If we ask a zoologist about a cat, for instance, he can tell us about its typical body structure and activities. If we ask why the cat exists, he replies by listing the ecological conditions which have to be fulfilled in order for a cat to survive. If we ask why those conditions are fulfilled, all the scientist can say is that as a matter of fact they do happen to be fulfilled. If we press him for further explanation, he will point out to us that the world happens to be made up in a certain way, with particular kinds of materials and energies which happen to interact according to certain regular patterns to produce our world. With these kinds of observations we come to the end of what the natural scientist can say about the matter, but in no way have we come to the end of our questions. We can point out aspects of these things which the natural scientist cannot explain and we can ask questions about them.

In these Jack-in-the-box and Jill-in-the-box questions we begin to recognise that the things in the world are like tracks. When Robinson Crusoe found the mark in the sand he did not rest easy with the thought that the grains of sand 'just happened to be in the shape of a footprint as a matter of fact for no reason or cause'. No! He quite intelligently and reasonably understood that the order in the grains of sand meant that it was a track made by a foot. Our understanding here follows the same course.

There just happen to be these particular kinds of materials and energies in the world rather than none at all, or completely different kinds. They just happen to follow these natural laws rather than none or others. The parts just happen to have come together to form stable arrangements so as to give a universe with levels (sub-atomic, atomic, molecular; sun, earth, moon; inorganic, plant, animal, human), rather than utterly different levels or none at all. All the bits and pieces just happen to have fallen together to form the incredibly ordered universe in which we live. These are the data of our experience: a world process in which certain kinds of materials and energies happen to exist and just happen to follow certain natural laws; in which stable rhythmical arrangements just happen to produce a series of levels of order each with cyclical patterns of activity; in which each lower level just happens to provide just the right conditions for the emergence, functioning and continuance of each higher level. The climate of opinion dominated by the closed view of the human person steps in at this point and tries to block the inquiry: "This is as far as you can go!" Are you aware of this interference from the climate of opinion? Well, you are a free human person, so you can stop at that point if you choose. If not, we can continue.

We can go further. How? By asking further questions. Why is there anything at all? Why is there not just nothing? Why does the whole process of reality exist? Why is it that the things which exist are the way they are and not some other way? Why are there these particular materials and energies? Why not other kinds? Why do the things that exist have the structures that they do have? Why don't they have completely different structures or no structure at all? To those who reply that the things developed in that way because of the way in which the whole process of reality unfolded, we address the further question: why did the process of reality unfold in this way rather than in some other way, or not at all? Why is it that stable arrangements and levels happen and survive? Why is there not only chaos?

Usually we try to push these questions back to a beginning. But at that point we have to take care because our imagination tends to offer confusing pictures. In any event, the pushing back of the inquiry to the beginning only serves to underline the utter inexplicableness of the whole process of reality; for if we say that the order at any point is due to the conditions which existed just before that moment, that explanation is not available to us at the beginning. If we go back to a moment of supposed simplicity before all the process had begun to unfold, we ask further questions. Why was there any stuff there at all to make a process with? Where did it come from? Why was it the kind of stuff that could produce the process of reality we happen to have rather than some other kind? Why did it begin to change and develop into our process of reality? Why did it not stay as it was or go some other way? It just shows you! They said we could not go any further. Behold! There are further questions and very interesting and important they seem to be!

These Jack-in-the-box and Jill-in-the-box questions indicate to us that the things in the world are like tracks; they are not totally self-explanatory or explicable in terms of other things in the world.

In this piece of knowing, as in any other, the questioning of our

137

experience leads to the occurrence of an act of understanding. As Robinson Crusoe leapt to the conclusion that what made the footprint was a foot, so we understand that the things in the world are tracks left by Something out of this world! This is by no means a full understanding of that Something: it is nothing more than the discovery that there is Something behind everything. As yet we have not got the slightest notion what that Something is like: all we have understood is that where there are tracks there is a track-maker.

As in any other piece of knowing, when we express what we have understood that sets off in us the desire to verify, to discover whether what we have understood is correct or whether it was just a possibility that turned out to have no foundation in reality. So, as soon as we have understood that "Something out of this world is!" we go on to ask whether this suggestion is true. Does this Something really exist? As before, we have to resist the mischievous play of imagination which throws up the picture of us opening a little door in the side of our head and stretching out of the world to take 'a look' to see whether this Something is really there. Checking and verifying is not like this at all. It is a matter of working out what conditions would have to be fulfilled if the suggestion were to be correct, and then discovering whether those conditions are in fact fulfilled. If the grains of sand are in that order, then a foot made them; but they are in that order; therefore a foot made them, a foot exists.

What, then, are the conditions which have to be fulfilled if Something out of this world exists?

i   If the things in the world exist, but their existence is not necessary, if their existing is intelligible, but not totally self-explanatory or explicable in terms of other things in the world, then their existence is caused by Something out of this world.

ii   If the things in the world have a certain structure, but this structure is not necessary, if this structure is intelligible, but not totally self-explanatory or explicable in terms of other things in the world, then their structure is caused by Something out of this world.

iii If the things in the world change, but this change is not necessary, if the change is intelligible but not totally self-explanatory or explicable in terms of other things in the world, then the change is caused by Something out of this world.

iv   If the things in the world are in a certain order, but this order is not necessary, if the order is intelligible but not totally self-explanatory or explicable in terms of other things in the world, then that order is caused by Something out of this world.

When we examine the things in the world in the light of these conditions it dawns on us that the conditions are fulfilled. To grasp this we have to keep in mind what is meant by necessary and by totally self-explanatory or explicable in terms of other things in the world. Necessary means something that cannot be other than it is, something that cannot not be: totally self-explanatory or explicable in terms of other things in the world, means that while there are some questions about things that the natural scientist can answer, there are others that he cannot. When we grasp that $1+1=2$, we understand that this relationship is necessary. When we understand that the cat is on the mat, we understand that this is not necessary. Ask a scientist what gravity is and he will reply: $g=981$ cms/sec/sec. Ask him why it is not a changing acceleration and why it has one numerical value rather than another, beyond a certain point he has to say that certain relationships happen to exist and that he cannot say why they have the form or value that they in fact have. It is in this sense that gravity and the other aspects of the universe are said to be not totally self-explanatory or explicable in terms of other things in the world: it means that we can raise valid questions which natural science cannot answer. We thus reach the conclusion:

The things in the world exist, have a certain structure, change and are in a certain order, but their existence, structure, change and order are not necessary: their existence, structure, change and order are intelligible, but not totally self-explanatory or explicable in terms of other things in the world: therefore, the existence, structure, change and order of the things in the world are caused by Something out of this world, Something which really is!

As Robinson Crusoe could work out a little about the foot by examining the footprint, so we could work out a little about this Something by examining the things in the world: but that is another day's journey. For the moment, it is enough that we be clear about how little we have discovered. We have not discovered *what* this Something is, only *that* it is. We have not studied It directly; we have only studied the tracks It left. What we have to say about It is that It cannot have the limitations which prevented the things in the world from being totally self-explanatory. Thus, we have to say that there is in It, no limit or change, no development or material. And since we are among the tracks It made, It must be spirit.

It is spirit, thus, infinite in understanding and love; Its understanding is the source of the intelligibility of the things in the world; the choice of Its love is the source of their very existence.

As this dawns upon us we are torn by a giant leap of the heart. The human heart responds to the mind's discovery of each new being with a quiet outburst of affectionate acceptance. Here, however, we have discovered Being which is infinite and personal. A soft supernova of acceptance explodes within us: we fall in love as never before — utterly, recklessly, with complete self-abandonment!

We realise with awe the outlandish kind of beings we are: now we glimpse what we are for. Each of us as a human person is a pure capacity to know and love being: but precisely because it is a pure capacity, none of the things in the world is immense enough to fill it. What, we asked, could fill an infinite capacity for understanding and love? Now we glimpse a possible answer. A Being in which there is an infinite actuality of understanding and love! We are for that Being as emptiness is for fullness. Other beings we know and love and that brings us a partial and passing fulfilment: but if only we could know and love that Being our fulfilment would be full, final and forever!

IT'S YOU!

A few memories haunt the imagination: all of a sudden they are stirred awake and well up again, carried by a quiet, deep outburst of the heart. When such a memory surfaces it sends out a ripple of breath-taking emotion, not massive at all, but fleeting, gentle, delicate, like a moment of extraordinary sensitivity or responsiveness. What remains is an eerie aftertaste, a poignant sense of significance incompletely grasped. I recall them as moments made unique and vivid, sacred and moving by the presence of . . . And that is the strange part: when I examine these memories they seem to contain nothing out of the ordinary. Why are these branded on my heart like few others? What presence consecrates them? Something weird my way passed and Its shadow touched me. Weird, because I saw or heard nothing! As if an invisible good giant had been there for an instant and had moved me in some way, so that some detail of whatever I happened to be doing or sensing at the time became associated in my heart and mind, my emotions and memory, with its visitation! Thereafter that detail remains vividly imprinted in me and from time to time, without my summoning it, the memory of it surfaces in my consciousness and brings with it this effusion of joy and affection, longing and heart's ease.

In one of these earliest memories I am picking apples with my father in the garden of the first house we lived in: I was less than three years old. I am climbing among the branches. A bucket on a rope. The apples are put into the bucket and let down. It is so good to be there with him. Within his arms' reach, under his gaze. In another, we listen enraptured to our mother while she tells us tales of Teacup and Tray, two dogs, as we eat sandwiches filled with mashed banana and jam. In another I sit on her knee and she tells the story of Ali Baba and the Forty Thieves. To be with her and to have her undivided attention! Whenever these memories return to mind a solemnity takes hold of me, and an affection so intense that it blurs the border-line between ecstasy and anguish. Often when they return I draw into myself spontaneously in an act of recollection: a shadow of majesty falls across me and discloses me to myself as ash before Its presence, but ash beloved.

It was here, too, from my father and mother in childhood, that I first heard of You and was taught to address You! And, of course, this Something out of this world that we are for, It's You! You are my invisible good giant. Those amazingly moving memories are of moments when You made Your presence felt to me and some detail of what was also present, a detail that faintly reflected You, was indelibly imprinted upon my memory. And sometimes when You manifest Your presence to me again, these memories return. What, then, am I for? I am for You! A human person is an infinite emptiness longing to be filled with You!

RELIGION

Stones and stars, plants and animals, just exist without asking what their existence means or what they are for. They have not within them that which would enable or allow them to take up an attitude towards their existence and its Source. We are different. We are able to ask what we are and to go in search of adequate answers. We wonder what we are for. We realise that we are unfinished beings who are called upon to take part in the work of completing and guiding their own development. We realise, also, that what we do shapes the way we develop. This sparks off in us the desire to discover what we are for, so that we can direct our knowing and loving in the right way, so that we can reach our natural and proper end as human persons. Every choice we make, no matter how small, and every deed we do, embodies and strengthens our basic life-choice, which is either to live in accordance with what we are, or not to do so.

I have discovered that I am for You. You are the natural and proper end of me as a human person. The only attitude that makes sense in this situation is the choice of You, the decision to go to You, my origin and end. The word 'religion' is much misunderstood today because the human spirit is not understood. But we have come at last upon its real meaning. It is said to come from the Latin *religare*, which means to bind fast, and especially, to fasten a ship to the shore: *ligare* means to bind, and the *re-* means 'again' and 'in a new and better way'. Religion, then, means this basic human activity of a person who has discovered You as the origin and end of their life, and who, as a result, takes up a new, deliberate and free attitude towards You, an attitude of self-donation, of binding ourselves with our heart's free choice to You to Whom we are already bound by the very thrust of our humanity. You have made us for You by giving us as the core of our personhood a capacity to know and love that can be satisfied by nothing other than You: but You leave it up to us to discover that we are for You and to freely choose to go to You, or not, as we decide.

In this journey to the Centre of the person I set off in search of my real name, my secret identity. Now, I discover that like the earth, the centre of whose movement lies outside it in the sun, the Centre of the human person is not itself, but You. My real name, my secret identity, is Yes to You. And my basic life-choice is this: open to You or closed to You?

THE UNIVERSAL ROMANCE

The nature of the human person is such that whatever we know, we love. As soon as we discover You, we love You, too. But, of course, we do not normally discover You in such a long-drawn-out, heavy-headed manner as presented here. Usually we do it more quickly, more intuitively, without putting into words all the steps and implications of our insight. We behold the day, and the light is hint enough for us to discover the Light behind it; we behold the growth of plant or animal, and in that life we discover also that other Life; in the warm love of our parents we discern also that other Parental Love. How do we know You? Who could count the ways! The analysis presented in the preceding pages merely makes explicit the marvellous moment of discovery common to people of all times and places wherein they leap from some of the things in the world to that Something else, out of this world, to You.

Once we have discovered You and grasped that it is for You alone that we are made, that only You are immense enough to match the scale and reach of the human spirit's longing, we begin to wonder what the meaning of our lives can be. We are for You, but we are unable to reach You directly yet because You are pure Spirit whereas we are little embodied spirits who are unable to know or love anything unless it is presented to us through our senses. Once asked, however, our minds get to work on the question and soon come up with the answer that our life is a journey to You. We do not see the end until we finish the journey: death seems to be the end of life's journey, so we guess that after death we may be with You.

It takes quite a while for us to become familiar with the way everything looks from this new viewpoint: it is only slowly that the implications of our openness to You and Your drawing of us towards You dawn on us. Gradually we realise that if I am an incarnate spirit of infinite capacity for being moved to understand and love, and You are infinitely understanding, loving, powerful Spirit, then I am for You, and my life in the world is a romance. My life is like a journey, a game, a trial, a quest, in which I have to seek You out and approach You, prepare myself to be with You. This is not so just for me but for every human person in the universe. As this way of understanding my life becomes habitual and engrained in me and drives out the closed view of the person and the world, I find that I am moving into a wider world, a kinder cosmos: as I overcome the denial of my own infinite potency and Your presence and care, I leave a prison in which I have been both prisoner and keeper, and enter the universal romance.

I remember watching television programmes about evolution in which the narrator, having presented the most beautiful and complex beings and interactions, commented that they represented yet another victory for random variation and chance. It crossed my mind at the time that far from looking like the outcome of accidental chance occurrences, the whole process of evolution resembled nothing more than a brilliant play or plot. It has a definite direction. And while I agree that it is not for natural science to jump in understanding from the direction to the Director, the natural scientist as a human person may well do so. What strikes me about the process of evolution is that it has a blatant direction, a drive from simple to more complex life-forms: and it is equally obvious to me that this process heads towards us! Granted, it is not a necessary process: the scientists are right when they say that it might have gone a million, million other ways. But it did not: it went only one way, and that way led to us! We are the stars of the show! What, then, is the point of the whole incredible affair?

You are the Director: You wrote the script. What are You up to? You have arranged the whole world like a vast treasure hunt. Every moment we meet things and people to know and love: these are the clues we must follow to reach the treasure. All the world's beauties and marvels, all its attractions and disappointments, everything invites us to raise the Jack-in-the-box and Jill-in-the-box questions that lead us to discover You. You made us and placed us in this world crammed with exquisite beauty, to awaken and whet our appetite for more: You made it all tantalizingly unsatisfactory in order to prevent us from resting contented with it. And every now and again, You peep out from behind the scenes and manifest Your presence to us so as to entice us to continue this game of Hide and Seek with You.

The things and people we know and love in the world are the words of a love letter: all the world's a love letter . . . The gift we receive from the one who loves us, first catches our attention by its own beauty: then, slowly, it draws us to realise that this other person gave it to us; finally, it brings us to wonder why, and to discover and, perhaps, to return in kind, their love for us. In the same way, the things and people we meet are gifts and letters of love written to us and left for us to find and absorb. You want us to discover that You sent them, and that You love us and want us to love You in return. Everything in the universe is there to play its part in the universal romance in which You conduct Your long and patient courtship of us: the meaning of each and every person's existence is this exchange of love in which You woo us one by one, by name.

Once I recognise the extent of Your preparation and care, I am struck by the contrast between my inattentiveness to You and Your relentless, unswerving, never-suspended-for-a-moment attentiveness to me. You leave me free at every point to say yes or no to You. In Your courtesy You refrain from coercion. You manifest Your presence and care now and again just to remind me that You are always there waiting in the wings for a few moments of my time. As soon as I begin to respond to Your gentle invitation, You start to play a mysterious game with me. Every time I take a step towards You, You seem to take a step back away from me, thus luring me ever deeper into the dark forest of Your friendship.

SECOND CHILDHOOD

One of the springs from which this journey grew was a fierce longing for the fullness and integrity represented by childhood. The ways of living imposed on us today in the name of adulthood deform and contract most of what we are as human persons. There must, I felt, be something more to human existence and maturity than the small-talk that currently poses as adult normality. I went in search of second childhood. Now I have found just that, a second childhood, for what earthly reality more adequately hints at the depth and detail of Your care and affection for me than parenthood? As the child is from the parent, only more so, am I from You. As the child is completely in the hands of the parent, only more so, am I in the palm of Your hand. As the child knows no joy greater than the presence and attention of the parent, so too, only more so, is Your presence and attention my greatest joy. The child loves above all to be at home: after a while away, homesickness pulls him back. So, too, You have skewered me with a harpoon of Homesickness that bids me draw nearer to You heart-beat by heart-beat.

I watched a newborn baby recently. His eyes wandered about from one thing to another. Then his mother sat him on her knee and searched his face with her eyes. He noticed his mother's face and their eyes met. His mother's face lit up in a radiant smile of love for him and joy in his being. Then, the little miracle! His face lit up in a happy sparkling smile: he wriggled and flapped his arms and gurgled a message of welcome recognition for her! She replied in his language. Later, I watched the same game being played between the child and his father and again, with the grandparents, the mutual searching of faces and the exchange of smiles. What a fabulous way to be welcomed into the world! Something akin to this happens when You make Yourself present to me. My heart goes out to You. It is not a seeing with the eye, nor a possession with the emotions, for You are my invisible good giant. Nor is it direct knowing, because You slip away so quickly and quietly that I have no chance to examine You. All I experience is the moment of the heart's surrender and the ripple of affection that accompanies it. In that moment I fall in love with You.

This fall into love for You plunges my heart to a depth within, of which I had never suspected myself possible; and it remains. The centre of gravity of my character remains anchored at that abysmal depth and sets in motion a lifelong re-ordering of mind and heart, of deed and habit, of feeling, fantasy and fidelity. Being in love with You remains the underlying state of my living.

One of the most powerful of those strange memories that stand out from my childhood is a scene from a comic-book version of Jules Verne's *The Mysterious Island*. In the tale, our heroes are stranded on an island and on several occasions they are saved from dangers by the interventions of a hidden stranger. The picture that impressed itself so vividly upon my memory was of a hand coming around a corner, the hand of the hidden helper! The more I become accustomed to the huger horizon that opens all about me once I throw off the confines of the closed view of the world and the person, the more I begin to recognise, as it were, Your hand around every corner. Sometimes I walk the children to school in the morning, one on either side of me. If I stretch out my hands to them, without drawing their attention to what I am doing, they spontaneously reach up their hands to grasp mine. May it be like this between You and me, may I leave my hand in Yours with the trust and abandonment of second childhood.

CONCLUSION

RECOLLECTION

We recognise now that what we have been engaged upon is a journey within the Journey to You. In our day, You have been largely eclipsed by the closed view of the world and the person. Ours, then, has been a journey to re-discover the Journey. The end of the journey is not the end of the Journey but a pause of recollection to gather up what we have discovered along the way. Perhaps the clearest way to put it is in the form of a list showing the main characteristics of the human person as they have emerged from our exploration, and for contrast, a blacklist, showing the dominant opinions about these characteristics from the closed viewpoint.

THE OPENNESS OF THE HUMAN PERSON

1. *Human knowing is open.*
Human knowing is able to go beyond what we sense or perceive, feel or want, beyond what we think might be or could be, to discover what really, truly and actually is, to know reality, to reach being.

2. *Human love is open.*
Human love is able to go beyond what gives me pleasure or what suits my interests, to accept what is found to exist, to love things in and for themselves. Human love is proportionate: it is able to discover the relationships between things and so to love them in the right way, to the right extent and in the right order.

3. *Human action is open.*
Human knowing is able to discover not merely what would give me pleasure or suit my interests here and now, but also what I ought to do: and human choice and action are able to choose freely to act according to that objective practical moral judgement.

4. *The human person is open.*

In the human person, as well as the body which we can see, there is the spirit which we cannot see. In the human spirit are capacities to know and love being. None of the things or people in the world are able to bring full, final and lasting fulfilment to the human person. The human spirit is a capacity to be moved to infinite knowing and loving: only in knowing and loving infinite Being could this spirit find full, final and lasting fulfilment. You are infinite Being. The human person, thus, is for You.

THE CLOSED VIEW OF THE HUMAN PERSON

1. *Human knowing is closed.*

Human knowing, according to the closed view, is unable to go beyond what we sense or perceive, feel or want, beyond what we think might be or could be. We are enclosed within our minds: all we know are our own opinions: what really exists, we have no way of discovering at all.

2. *Human love is closed.*

Human love, according to the closed view, is unable to go beyond what gives me pleasure or suits my interests. Human love is closed in selfishness. The word good has no other meaning whatever than what gives me pleasure or suits me. What is really good, we have no way of discovering at all.

3. *Human action is closed.*

Human knowing is unable to go beyond what gives me pleasure or suits my interests to discover what I ought to do here and now. And human action is not able to do anything other than what gives me pleasure or suits my interests. What I really ought to do here and now, I simply am unable to discover or do, according to the closed view.

4. *The human person is closed.*

When all is said and done, as far as the closed view is concerned, the human person is really just another kind of animal. If there is something in us called knowing and loving and responsible action, it is closed within the world and within its own inescapable selfishness. The world is all there is and nothing exists beyond it: or if it does, we can know nothing about it and it has nothing to do with us. Certainly, we are in no real sense infinite in any way, nor are we primarily for anything out of this world. Emphatically, the closed view insists, we are part and parcel of the world and we must find whatever satisfaction we can in the things and people in the world.

These, then, are two ways of understanding what we are. According to the open understanding of the person, you have a mind of your own and can explore your own experience to discover which of these descriptions is true to it; you are, furthermore, free, and so you can choose if you wish to try to live according to whichever account you like. According to the closed view, you cannot go beyond opinions about the human person to discover what you really are, nor can you do other than what gives you pleasure or suits your interests. I have tried to show that the closed view rests on an inadequate understanding of the human spirit and its capacity to know and love. As we leave behind the closed view of the person and the world we rediscover our earthlikeness: we are starlight housed in clay and centred on pure starfire. We are Stardust, the host of humankind, hurtling headlong Homewards into You.

ACKNOWLEDGEMENTS

I wish to thank my wife, Gemma, for long-term endurance of a husband distracted by study. Thank you for that, but much more, Gemma, thank you for coming into my life and enriching it.

I wish to thank Fr. Brendan Purcell who has directed my work over the past fifteen years. The vision in these pages is to a large extent the fruit of his teaching and our conversation. Thank you Bren.

I wish to thank Bruno and the community for practical help of every kind, but more for the life of unity and the gift of the Ideal.

And I wish to thank James O'Connor for his help — without it this book would never have been published, but more for his friendship and *joie de vivre*: their trace is in these pages. Thanks James.

Finally, I wish to thank Niall O'Carroll for technical advice and assistance. Thanks Niall.